APOCA-
LYPSE
NOT

APOCA-
LYPSE
NOT

Science, Economics, and Environmentalism

Ben Bolch and Harold Lyons

CATO
INSTITUTE
Washington D.C.

Library of Congress Cataloging-in-Publication Data

Bolch, Ben W., 1938–
    Apocalypse not : science, economics, and environmentalism / Ben
Bolch and Harold Lyons.
        p.   cm.
    Includes bibliographical references and index.
    ISBN 1-882577-05-1 (cloth) : $19.95.—ISBN 1-882577-04-3 (pbk.) :
$10.95
    1. Environmental degradation. I. Lyons, Harold. II. Title.
GE140.B64   1993   93-19348
363.7—dc20   CIP

Cover Design by Colin Moore.

Printed in the United States of America.

CATO INSTITUTE
1000 Massachusetts Ave., N.W.
Washington, D.C. 20001

Contents

Preface

Since its founding in 1970 and by its own estimate, the Environmental Protection Agency has imposed some $1.4 trillion in compliance costs on the American economy.[1] Hazardous waste costs have escalated to the point where it is estimated that in one instance $15 billion was spent to avoid a single cancer.[2] For Superfund, the fund that is supposed to ensure against harm from hazardous waste disposal, the vast majority of money spent (probably over 80 percent) goes to legal fees and the like.[3] The Office of Management and Budget has calculated that an EPA rule on wood preservatives has a projected cost per early death prevented that is approximately equal to the current GNP of the United States ($5.7 trillion).[4]

Economists now routinely include environmental regulation costs in their explanations of why the growth rate of the American economy has slowed in recent years, and traditional scientists complain about the diversion of research funds into trendy environmental projects and away from research they believe would have a more beneficial impact on humanity. When environmental issues are involved, the press loses its traditional skepticism and blindly reports the ravings of the most outlandish doomsayer as if those words were holy writ.

To say that the scientific community is in great disagreement over the environmental issues treated in this book is a gross understatement. For example, despite the media's treatment of global warming as fact, Philip Abelson, editor of *Science*, the prestigious journal of the American Association for the Advancement of Science, used the word "hype" in a lead editorial about the issue in

[1]Peter Brimelow and Leslie Spencer, "You Can't Get There from Here," *Forbes*, July 6, 1992, p. 59.

[2]Philip H. Abelson, "Remediation of Hazardous Waste Sites," *Science*, February 21, 1992, p. 901.

[3]"Environmentalism Runs Riot," *Economist*, August 8, 1982, p. 11.

[4]Ibid.

March 1990. If the models that predict a warmer future are correct, common sense tells us that they should also work in reverse—they should give an accurate characterization of the climate in, say, 1890. Since they do not, are we not correct in being skeptical of them?[5]

When scientific work does not agree with the current environmental dogma, such work is often buried, as was the case of the $400 million acid rain report commissioned by the U.S. government. That report questioned whether acid rain was a major problem. The difficulty with the study is that it appeared when the Bush administration was seeking to push through the Clean Air Act of 1990. In a similar way the environment secretary of Brazil was sacked when he suggested—10 weeks before the 1992 Rio environmental conference—that if industrialized nations were willing to give billions of dollars to the Third World for environmental projects, those funds would simply be swallowed up by corrupt governments.[6] Environmentalists do not suffer reasoned opposition lightly.

We decided to write this book because we came to understand that much of the modern environmental movement is a broad-based assault on reason and, not surprisingly, a concomitant assault on freedom. Assaults on freedom are always accompanied by assaults on reason, and anyone who becomes convinced that common sense is no longer a reliable guide to living becomes prey to charlatans of every kind. So it has been in the past and will continue to be in the future: people who would preserve freedom must be steadfast in their belief in reason.

Prefaces are places for giving thanks, and no author is ever short on indebtedness. To our wives, Anne and Helen, goes our greatest gratitude. Our students, Steve Sullivan, Bill Jordan, and Vickie Edrington, gave an extraordinary amount of assistance in checking sources and facts. Lynne Blair and Annette Cates of Rhodes' Library were, as always, cheerful and invaluable. Marci Hendrix provided excellent proofreading and typing skills.

[5]See S. Fred Singer, "No Scientific Consensus on Greenhouse Warming," *Wall Street Journal*, September 23, 1991, p. A6.
[6]See "Brazil's Greens Shoot the Pianist," *Economist*, March 28, 1992, p. 38.

We also thank the editors of *Public Interest* for permission to reprint (with minor changes and additions) chapter 5, "A Multibillion-Dollar Radon Scare," which first appeared in the Spring 1990 issue of that publication.

Even though we are by training an economist and a chemist, this book is not about either of those subjects. Rather it is an effort of a social scientist and a natural scientist to pool resources in an attempt to understand the great modern hysteria that we call the environmental movement. It is also about two good friends who have had a fine time working together.

B. B. and H. L.
Memphis, 1992

1. The Environment and Environmentalism

It is surely true that the environment is one of the most widely discussed issues of the day. In the face of large amounts of programming devoted to matters ecological by public and private television networks, the spate of companies (down to local carpet cleaners) that now advertise their products as "environmentally safe," and the reams of junk mail people receive from environmentalist groups peddling some new object of salvation, we cannot fail to wonder whether the environmental movement is merely another fad on a long list that has been adopted by our fad-prone culture. But there is more to the environmental movement than mere faddism. To paraphrase the great American linguist and philosopher Irving Babbitt, when the environmental problem is looked at with any degree of thoroughness, an economic problem will emerge, under which will be found a political problem, below which will emerge a philosophical problem, all of which will finally be undergirded by a religious problem.[1]

Environment, Economics, Politics, Philosophy, and Religion

The desire to preserve the environment, like any other, implies a willingness to sacrifice. Economists will tell you that if, for example, cleaner air is desired, something else will, implicitly or explicitly, have to be given up. These concessions might include increased prices for certain goods; decreased income; or the absence of entire classes of goods, services, or freedoms. Further, these sacrifices tend to increase exponentially as greater environmental purity is sought: everyone who has done laundry knows that the cost of

---

[1]Irving Babbitt, *Democracy and Leadership* (1924. Reprint. Indianapolis: Liberty Classics, 1979), p. 23. The original quotation is: "When studied with any degree of thoroughness, the economic problem will be found to run into the political problem, the political problem in turn into the philosophical problem, and the philosophical problem itself to be almost indissolubly bound up at last with the religious problem."

removing obvious filth from a pair of jeans is relatively low in comparison to the cost of rendering the jeans sterile enough to use as surgical dressing.

Yet the cost of environmental improvements seems not to have sunk into the minds of voters and consumers. There are probably many reasons for this lack of understanding, but the most obvious one that comes to mind is America's growing political attitude that government can somehow solve this and other problems at reduced (or even zero) cost. The rhetoric of the politician who promises to take the cost of environmental improvement out of the hide of the evil polluter without touching the voter or the consumer is, of course, as much economic nonsense as the idea that real wages can be increased by government edict without causing increased unemployment. The relevant question for any politician concerns methods that the government might apply to bring environmental quality to an acceptable level at the least cost to the consumer. Put another way, if we are lucky, we might find a truly clever politician who could deliver $1.00 worth of environmental improvement to consumers at a cost of only $1.00 rather than, say, $50.00.

All of which brings us to philosophical problems concerning ethics, morals, and the like. Do animals have rights, and if so, what are they? Should nature itself have standing in courts of law? How dare an economist purport to assign a cost to something of untold value, such as a wetland?

A story that has found its way into the lore of environmental economics illustrates the interplay of philosophy with economics and politics—the case of the Cayman Turtle Farm, Ltd.[2] The green sea turtle is considered endangered. In an attempt to protect it, some very unpopular measures have been legislated, such as forcing Gulf Coast shrimpers to use a type of net that is detrimental to their shrimp harvesting. In response to the turtle shortage, a company was formed in the late 1960s to cultivate turtles. The enterprise was quite successful: large quantities of turtles were bred in captivity and an increasing number were marketed. Nevertheless, the project met with much hostility from a great many environmentalists who felt that it was morally wrong to "exploit" the turtles

[2]See Robert J. Smith, "Private Solutions to Conservation Problems," in *The Theory of Market Failure*, ed. Tyler Cowen (Fairfax, Va.: George Mason University Press, 1988).

for profit. Their solution was to ban the sale of turtle products completely.

By the late 1970s, the U.S. departments of Commerce and Interior had acquiesced to the clamor of the environmentalists and had banned the importation of turtle products into the United States— an act that helped spell the end of the Cayman Turtle Farm experiment. Here the philosophical position that sea turtles "should not be exploited" won the day over the sentiments of even such worthies as Jacques Yves Cousteau, who is quoted to have said, "If the sea turtle is to survive, it must be farmed."[3]

One wonders just how many domestic cattle would exist in the United States if commerce in these animals were banned. In the same way, many economists believe that banning commerce in certain animals may be one of the best ways to ensure their ultimate demise, for while such a ban may make a kind of animal worthless in legal commerce, it also makes the animal unlikely to be protected and nurtured by virtue of its very commercial worthlessness. Philosophical predilections against the trade of certain types of animals and their products may be completely misplaced as far as the welfare of the animal species is concerned.

Finally, we come to religion, which we will define in the sense of a cause or a belief subscribed to with fervor and faith. It is here that we come closer to understanding the essence of the environmental movement. All religious movements have essential tenets, and the main tenet of this movement is that the environment is being degraded by mankind rapidly and that only an elect can save *nature* from imminent catastrophe. Notice we did not say that mankind needs to be saved from catastrophe: mankind has increasingly become expendable to believers of this religion.

If modern environmentalism is akin to a religion, what is at first puzzling is the movement's apparent death wish for mankind and, we might add, for itself. The notion that technology needs to be abandoned, that farms need to be small and communal, or that trade among world economies is a sign of imbalance and must be prevented are all tenets of "deep ecology." Those tenets spell extinction by starvation and disease for millions of people on this planet. Indeed, the death wish has been made explicit in more than

[3]Ibid., p. 351.

one place, a letter to the publication *Earth First!* being perhaps the most notorious:

> The only way to stop all of the destruction of our home is to decrease the birth rate or increase the death rate of people. . . . It does no good to kill a few selected folks. That is a retail operation. . . . The simple expedient: biological warfare! Think about it. It fits. It is species specific. . . . Biological warfare will have no impact on other creatures, big or small, if we design it carefully.[4]

Of course, other examples of hatred for human beings are shown by the fringe of the environmental movement. Consider the description of AIDS as "a welcome development in the inevitable reduction of human population."[5] The message is clear that the human-centered religion and philosophy of the West must give way to a new religion that worships things like "the wilderness" for their own sake and not for any economic or even aesthetic benefit that they can give to mankind. One can certainly love the woodlands and still recoil from the ethics of ecoterrorists who carry out instructions in books such as *Ecodefense: A Field Guide to Monkey-wrenching* and put loggers' lives at risk by spiking trees so chain saws will be shattered. In fact, as a public protest grew to pass federal laws to prohibit tree spiking in the Northwest, the relative position of people and trees was made quite clear when an Earth First! leader reportedly said, "The old-growth forest of North Idaho is a hell of a lot more important than Joe Sixpack."[6]

Of course, most people who respect and revere nature (including ourselves) do not believe in deep ecology or ecoterrorism. But the

---

[4]Anonymous, untitled letter to the publication *Earth First!*, November 1, 1984, p. 3.

[5]As quoted in Michael Parfit, "Earth First!ers Wield a Mean Monkey Wrench," *Smithsonian*, April 1990, p. 198.

[6]Quoted in Dean Miller, "McClure Wants Federal Law against Tree-Spiking," *Spokane Review*, August 1, 1987, p. 1. Earth First! by no means represents the extreme of the environmental movement in the United States. By the late 1980s, Earth First! had begun to attract more militant anarchists such as Mike Jakubal, who with others has formed splinter groups that publish newspapers such as *Live Wild or Die*. Its first few issues featured articles on topics such as shoplifting and making free long-distance phone calls. Members of the "Gross Action Group," who have taken part in "Puke-Ins," are said to be an affront to the old-line members of Earth First! See Rick Scarce, *Eco-Warriors* (Chicago: Noble Press, 1990), p. 88.

fringes of a sect always seem to set the tone for more moderate believers, and mainstream environmentalists remain strangely quiet as the fringe moves inexorably toward lunacy. David Brower, who has held important official positions with both the Sierra Club and Friends of the Earth, not only refuses to condemn Earth First! but was quoted as saying: "Earth First! makes Friends of the Earth look reasonable. What we need now is an outfit that makes Earth First! look reasonable."[7]

Environmental Utopia

Sincere scholars who seek to understand the motives of the environmental movement disagree over whether it is at root a political-economic struggle for power or a manifestation of a new kind of religion: political scientist Aaron Wildavsky is a good exponent of the power theory[8] while economist Robert Nelson is a leading advocate of the religion theory.[9] We believe there are both elements in the environmental movement. Just as a kind of religion is mixed with the need for power in utopian systems such as Marxism, so religion and power are intertwined in the environmental movement. Indeed, by looking at the environmental movement as a form of utopianism, one has the best chance of understanding its complex, sometimes irrational, and often contradictory viewpoints.

The great psychologist Carl Jung wrote that utopia, or the dream of a Golden Age, is archetypal (that is, it is an imprint on the human psyche).[10] In this dream is the concept of a just and wise leader who by superior knowledge causes everything to be provided in abundance while at the same time permitting all persons to dwell within an atmosphere of peace, justice, equality, and even the Kingdom of God on Earth. But Jung goes on to state the obvious:

> The sad truth is that man's real life consists of a complex of inexorable opposites—day and night, birth and death,

[7]Doug Bandow, "Ecoterrorism: The Dangerous Fringe of the Environmental Movement," Heritage Foundation Backgrounder, April 12, 1990, p. 8.

[8]See Aaron Wildavsky, " 'Ecotheology' Is Liberal, Not Religious," *Policy Review*, Fall 1990, pp. 90–91.

[9]Robert H. Nelson, "Unoriginal Sin: The Judeo-Christian Roots of Ecotheology," *Policy Review*, Summer 1990, pp. 52–59.

[10]Carl G. Jung, "Approaching the Unconscious," in *Man and His Symbols*, ed. C. G. Jung and M.-L. von Franz (New York: Doubleday, 1964), p. 85.

happiness and misery, good and evil. We are not even
sure that one will prevail against the other, that good will
overcome evil, or joy defeat pain. Life is a battleground. It
always has been, and always will be; and if it were not so,
existence would come to an end.[11]

The environmental movement's similarities to utopian crusades
are fairly simple to detail by reference to Thomas Molnar's taxon-
omy of utopianism.[12] With reference to religion, there is often a
rejection of much of the Judeo-Christian heritage in both modern
socialist utopian moments and in extreme environmentalism. Environmentalism displays a special objection to the biblical injunction
for mankind to be fruitful and multiply and to hold dominion over
other creatures and Earth.[13] Along those same lines, environmentalism has more than a streak of pantheism (in the sense of the worship
of multiple manifestations of nature) and much of the notion of
deus absconditus, or the transcendent god knowable only to the elect.

Those same knowledgeable elect are, of course, to become rulers
of the new regime under both the socialist and environmental
utopia. And, as in Marxism, the elect are to be "scientific," but
only insofar as their interpretation of science fits the movement's
demands. Scientists who do not agree with the movement's dogma
are branded as inferior or second-rate, regardless of their training
or present position, and their opinions are disparaged. In both
utopian socialism and environmentalism, the responsibility of this
scientific elite is both to exterminate any "pseudoscientific" resis-
tance to the movement (through censorship, if needed) and to help
ensure that the educational system is used to internalize the proper
norms among present and future generations. As Molnar put it:

> The Elect, or the Utopian leaders, consider themselves pure
> or, at any rate, above those standards by which the rest of
> humanity is judged.[14]

---

[11]Ibid.

[12]Thomas Molnar, *Utopia, the Perennial Heresy* (1967. Reprint. Lanham, Md.: University Press of America, 1990).

[13]See the review by Jeanne Kay, "Human Dominion over Nature in the Hebrew
Bible," *Annals of the Association of American Geographers*, June 1989, pp. 214–32.

[14]Molnar, p. 193.

Modern socialist utopian movements, like much of the environmental movement, stress the need to look far into the future (as in the thousand-year Reich) and to impose great present sacrifices to ensure the goodness of the outcome of that distant future. This forward-looking stance of the environmental movement often leads to specious forecasts, such as those associated with global warming, where experts have the temerity to discuss the weather 50 years in the future when present-day weather forecasters have difficulty forecasting 50 days (much less 50 months) into the future. Nevertheless, those movements are willing, by virtue of their fantastic pretensions of knowledge, to grant colossal powers to the state. Such powers allow the control and manipulation of every detail of political, economic, and intellectual life for the sake of an improved future. An absurdly long time horizon, coupled with absolute state control, is supposed to ensure for both socialist utopians and environmentalists that the base selfishness in mankind will be replaced by a collective consciousness that is ever more favorable to the movement's goals.

Like the socialist utopian movements, the environmental movement places much emphasis on the absolute necessity for international acceptance. The need for planetary unity for environmentalism is constantly reinforced with prominent international meetings of scientists and show-business personalities, who are required to issue statements of solidarity with the cause or condemnation of opponents of the latest phase of the cause.

Anna Bramwell and others have drawn attention to the environmental movement's death wish.[15] Why would a movement advocate policies that have been characterized as nothing less than "A War against Fire"[16] and that would surely destroy itself and much of the world's population at the same time? The present size of the planet's population is predicated on the technology and market mechanisms now in place, and their destruction would destroy a large segment of mankind. We cannot return to a "small and beautiful" world, a tribal world free of the difficulties of modern society, because to do so would be suicide. Yet, as we find in reading the

[15]Anna Bramwell, *Ecology in the 20th Century: A History* (New Haven, Conn.: Yale University Press, 1989).

[16]Russell Seitz, "A War against Fire: The Uses of 'Global Warming,' " *National Interest*, Summer 1990, pp. 54–62.

literature on the religious aspects of utopian movements such as environmentalism, a death wish is far from uncommon.

Michael Novak, with characteristic clarity, explains the death wish best when he points out the elemental fact that utopian socialist movements are, at root, wars against individualism—they are crusades aimed at the elimination of the self. Such utopian movements are akin to romantic love, and like Romeo and Juliet, the myth of romantic love has perhaps its best ending in the glorious embrace of death. Furthermore,

> The privileged heroes of the socialist imagination are martyrs who die for the revolution. Not their success, but their self-immolation, is held in highest honor. For no one dares to say in what socialist success consists. . . . As its inner will is the wish for self-immolation, so it longs for death, in which every human being is uniform. . . . [Finally, some]. . . may be, for their own good, consigned to annihilation, in order to cleanse the earth.[17]

It is difficult to know how many people have adopted the environmental and Green movements as substitutes for national socialism or communism. Certainly the rhetoric and aims among those movements are similar, and that affinity will no doubt become clearer to people who observe the future evolution of the demands of the neo-utopian environmental fringe. But once these affinities become clear to a sufficient segment of the American people, a backlash against even sound environmental improvement will surely develop. That backlash will spell a tragic rejection of the efforts of hundreds of thousands of sincere people who have worked diligently for a better environment with no grander vision than, perhaps, to clean up a vacant lot or to police the shores of a local recreation lake.

The Synergy of Economics and Environmentalism

If, in the spirit of Babbitt, economic issues simply underpinned environmental ones, our task of separating the two would be eased to a considerable degree. But, as many people have pointed out

---

[17]Michael Novak, *Will it Liberate?: Questions about Liberation Theology* (New York: Paulist Press, 1986), pp. 194–5.

(including EPA administrator William Reilly[18]), the two are highly synergistic: the very definition of a good environment clearly depends on the standard of living of the people who live in that environment. Even the most rudimentary sanitary improvements must await an income level high enough to support them. The bulk of environmental discontent, even in the present-day United States, comes from people with property to protect against environmental problems such as noise and visual "pollution." The interesting complication is, therefore, that a society's perception of the "good" environment depends on its perception of what can be afforded. The difficulties, of course, are that dreams of what can be afforded usually outpace economic reality, and that all members of a society almost never have similar views on the economic reality itself.

The beauty of the pluralistic society that most Americans once cherished is that people who place great value on environmental amenities, and can afford them, are quite free to spend their own income to obtain them. The idea that a wealthy person could repair to some natural retreat at periodic intervals is an old one in our culture. In fact, Americans value the benefits of natural settings so greatly that the nation has extended the ability to return to those settings to the poor by providing public parks, seashores, and the like. Thus, in the late 19th and early 20th centuries, when the federal government spent a minuscule portion of national income by present standards, the Preservation movement was able to mobilize public opinion in favor of a system of national parks. But preservationists like John Muir were interested in the rewards to humanity of preserving the beauty of nature and in the intangible benefits (such as greater love of country) that natural preserves might bring in their train. Another great American movement, the Conservationists, was even more utilitarian, stressing such things as water projects and sustained agricultural yields. According to the great champion of that movement, Gifford Pinchot, "Conservation means the greatest good for the greatest number [of people] for the longest time."[19] Modern environmentalism is qualitatively very different from both of those earlier movements in that it seems to

[18]William K. Reilly, "The Green Thumb of Capitalism," *Policy Review*, Fall 1990, pp. 16–21.

[19]As quoted in Roderick Frazier Nash, *American Environmentalism: Readings in Conservation History*, 3d ed. (New York: McGraw-Hill, 1990), p. 69.

9

have forgotten the benefits that preservation and conservation can bestow on mankind; nature is to be protected from mankind, not to be used to mankind's benefit. People, in this view, are merely an intrusion on nature.

Environmentalist solutions are often to ban entire classes of activities (the production and use of DDT) and to view preservation of natural habitats in an abstract manner sometimes completely devoid of any aesthetic—much less economic—use by mankind (for example, the closing of easy access to public parks). Since items such as DDT have been of enormous benefit to mankind, and since many people wonder at the utility of supporting parks that do people little or no good, many programs of the environmental movement have been difficult to sell. In its zeal to sell extreme programs, the movement does itself and those who respect and love the natural world little good.

The Backlash

Subsequent chapters will point out several areas where the environmentalist's case has been based on science that is sometimes hardly worthy of being called shoddy. People who would sell those causes seem to have discovered that the public-relations expert and the attorney are more powerful (at least in the short run) than the scientist. In the long run, however, that mode of operation is sure to cause trouble. A backlash against people who cry wolf when no wolf is at hand is bound to occur, and we believe that it can be detected in many ways today. Apart from the defeat by voters in November 1990 of environmental measures of all kinds, including such extreme measures as California's "Big Green" proposition, a smaller but no less telling illustration may suffice. The PBS program "This Old House" is about restoring homes. In 1989 a program about asbestos removal from a structure met with the grave concern and approval of the program's hosts. Then a 1990 program described the removal of lead-based paint from the windows, doors, and baseboards of a Boston rental property. A team of experts diagnosed the extent of lead in the paint, and a member of a second team, who dubbed themselves "deleaders," then appeared, complete with white jump suits and respirators. That team covered the interior of the house with plastic sheets, constructed a decontamination room, and informed the show's hosts that the residue of paint that they were removing might be so dangerous as to need, by law, to be placed in a hazardous waste disposal site! The show's hosts were told that the cost would run to several thousand dollars. The spokesman for the deleaders was also quick to inform the hosts that a person had to be licensed to perform this dangerous operation in Boston. The irritation in the voices and on the faces of the hosts seemed evident.

That little story illustrates, in microcosm, the fears of people who worry about an increased environmental bureaucracy. A seemingly innocuous law is passed to control lead-based paint, but the law requires bureaucrats for its execution. Those bureaucrats, who have no financial stake in the outcome, regulate ever more tightly until remodeling itself becomes prohibitively expensive. Today, for example, some buildings in the United States stand in decay because their owners cannot afford the high cost of asbestos removal. As we will discuss in a later chapter, such removal is often counterproductive to public health.

Regulation in the housing industry has become so pervasive that Jack Kemp, former secretary of Housing and Urban Development, estimated that regulation (much of it environmental) in New Jersey accounted for 25–35 percent of the cost of a new home.[20] That regulation is certainly no friend of the poor.

Part of the backlash against environmentalism will come because of increasingly unreasonable environmental restrictions, which by now, in some jurisdictions in California, intrude into the operation of backyard barbecue grills. But another part of the backlash will come because of false predictions of environmental catastrophe. People will surely be more prone to ignore cancer warnings on substances that are clearly carcinogenic (such as cigarettes) when they are told that hundreds of common substances that they have eaten or ingested their entire lives are carcinogenic. People cannot fail to make the connection that the same people who prevented increased use of nuclear power for decades now cry that fossil fuels cause global warming. Americans are not so naive as to overlook the fact that they and their ancestors were able to live in a house

[20]Jack Kemp, "Free Housing from Environmental Snobs," *Wall Street Journal*, July 8, 1991, p. A10.

for a hundred years without contracting lung cancer, and yet are now told the house is unsafe because of radon.

Is There a Less Hysterical Case?

No doubt this book errs on the side of presenting the case for restraining people whose stock in trade is environmental hysteria. Our basic thesis is that the world is not about to come to an end and that by nearly any measure, the people who reside in the market-oriented economies of the West enjoy a cleaner and safer environment than ever experienced in modern history. Since the 1850s, the average life expectancy in the United States has nearly doubled, from around 40 years to around 80 years. The improvement has been so sweeping and dramatic that if we completely eliminated *all* mortality (every single death) before the age of 50, our life expectancy would increase by only 3.5 years.[21] We view that fact as the most dramatic proof imaginable that the environment has not deteriorated as far as human beings are concerned.

We believe that in our two years of research for this book, a growing segment of the scientific community has come to agree with our assessment that the earth is in no great danger of being poisoned. Nevertheless, this side of the environmental story is not being told, because there is no money to be made in telling it. Hysteria sells newspapers, enrolls members in environmental protection groups, allows bureaucrats to increase their power, and creates markets for corrective measures in a way that the *Wall Street Journal* calls a zero-sum game: money is taken from organizations like electric utilities and shunted toward organizations that claim to improve the environment.[22] But zero-sum games are not the stuff of economic growth and long-run improvement in standards of living.

We hold great reverence for nature, for the American economy, and for the integrity of science. We see the environmental mania as a destructive force in each of those areas. It is clear to any impartial observer that some environmental laws and restrictions

---

[21]S. Jay Olshansky et al., "In Search of Methuselah: Estimating the Upper Limits of Human Longevity," *Science*, November 2, 1990, pp. 634–40.

[22]Rose Gutfeld, "For Each Dollar Spent on Clean Air Someone Stands to Make a Buck," *Wall Street Journal*, October 29, 1990, p. 1.

are harming both the economy and our ability to compete internationally, but what is rarely mentioned is that some of those laws are so poorly thought out and drafted that they are actually harming the environment as well. And when scientists resort to overt falsehoods and distortions to sell environmental programs, such activity will eventually destroy the integrity of science itself.

Of course, we have not addressed many issues; we deal with others only briefly. The question of possible harmful effects of electromagnetic fields is one of the current hot (pun intended) environmental issues but one that seems to lack any credible scientific evidence on either side. Therefore, we will treat that subject but briefly. Despite the lack of evidence, power companies are investing huge sums of money to research methods of reducing electromagnetic fields in the fear that reductions will be imposed on them by the regulators or the courts. Interestingly, those companies are in a "Catch-22"; if they do discover ways to reduce the fields, they will probably be forced to do so whether or not any adverse effects from the fields are ever shown. Such is the fear, in that industry, of environmentalists and their lawyers.

We will not talk about deforestation and associated loss of biodiversity. First, nobody seems to know how much forest has been damaged in countries such as Brazil, much less how much of an effect this injury has had on biodiversity: the Brazilian Institute for Space Research has an estimate of damaged forest area using Landsat satellite data. The estimate is about half as large as the typically published figure.[23] Second, much of the abusive use of forests is abetted by state actions (as in Brazil), and a major theme of this book is that such state actions should not be tolerated. Third, we have concentrated our attention on the United States. Here the endangered species laws appear to block economic development quite handily—excessively so, as many loggers who are now unemployed because of an owl might say.

For other omissions, we apologize in advance. No book, especially a small one, can cover all present and emerging issues of environmentalism, and certainly no book can please everyone in such a divisive and value-laden field of inquiry. To paraphrase

[23]The Institute's figure in 1990 was about 251,000 square kilometers as compared to an often cited figure of 598,000 square kilometers. See "Instant Trees," *Economist*, April 28, 1990, p. 93.

C. S. Lewis's comments concerning devils, we agree that there are two equal and opposite errors to be avoided when thinking about the environment.[24] One is to disbelieve that the environment matters at all. The other is to have an excessive and unhealthy interest in the environment. A way to avoid this unhealthy interest is surely needed.

[24]From the preface to his *Screwtape Letters* (New York: Bantam Books, 1982).

2. Rationality, Morality, and Environmentalism

A walk of a few minutes in the relatively dirty air of many Western European cities will convince anyone that the $30 billion or so (probably double that figure under the Clean Air Amendments of 1990) that the United States spends each year for clean air does have some effect. The almost pristine character of air in most U.S. cities is even more apparent when one considers the relative cleanliness of Western European cities as compared to those in many other parts of the world.

Nobody wants air polluted with ozone, streams contaminated with heavy metals, or food containing carcinogens. Nobody wants to see forests destroyed or animal species made extinct. Nobody wants thousands of people killed by automobiles each year, either. Yet, of this list of things nobody seems to want, only one thing can absolutely be prevented by society—deaths by automobile. The rest can and do occur naturally, with or without the consent or influence of human beings.

Society has seemingly made a calculation and has decided that it does not want to force deaths from automobile accidents to fall to zero persons per year. Otherwise, automobiles would be banned. Instead, a comparatively frightful toll in human life has been accepted as a cost of freedom of movement. Moreover, society has been willing to make only marginal adjustments in this tradeoff— a temporary change in the speed limit here, a safety feature there. Indeed, when Congress passed legislation to force the use of seat belts by mandating a seat belt–ignition interlock system, it was met with such howls of protest by the general public that the interlock (like Prohibition) became one of the few examples of federal government interference in private decisions ever to be repealed in the 20th century.

One certainly need not favor a dirtier environment to have serious questions about the rationality of the environmental movement.

For example, 80 percent of the people polled by the *New York Times* and CBS News in June 1989 agreed with the following statement: "Protecting the environment is so important that requirements and standards cannot be too tight, and continuing environmental improvements must be made regardless of the cost."[1] What did they mean? Were they posturing, were they intentionally giving the pollsters a witless answer to an inane question, or were they sincerely ignorant of the fact that zero pollution is impossible (and therefore infinitely costly) as long as there are any living things on earth? Why does it seem that the cleaner our environment becomes the more strident the environmental movement becomes? Perhaps Eric Hoffer had it right four decades ago in his book *The True Believer* when he said that for mass movements such as this: "The intensity of discontent seems to be in inverse proportion to the distance from the object fervently desired."[2]

What Is Risk?

There is little doubt that many people in the environmental movement have, as Robert Nelson ably points out, adopted an ecotheology.[3] Segments of the environmental movement such as Earth First! have taken on the ugly and sometimes violent militancy of a moral crusade—a return to religious inquisition, if you will. Risk assessment expert William Clark, for example, directly equates our increasing concern over environmental risk to witch-hunting.[4] Once a substance has been accused of being an environmental risk, there is nothing that can exonerate the substance and terminate investigation. If a substance is not a risk in parts per trillion, it can always be examined on a parts-per-billion basis: the search effort creates the thing being sought. Such methods of investigation are far from the careful and unbiased methods of science that have done so

[1]V. Kerry Smith, "Can We Measure the Economic Value of Environmental Amenities?" *Southern Economic Journal*, April 1990, pp. 865–78.

[2]Eric Hoffer, *The True Believer* (New York: Harper & Row, 1951), p. 28.

[3]Robert H. Nelson, "Unoriginal Sin: The Judeo-Christian Roots of Ecotheology," *Policy Review*, Summer 1990, pp. 52–59.

[4]William Clark, "Witches, Floods, and Wonder Drugs: Historical Perspectives on Risk Management," in *Societal Risk Assessment: How Safe Is Safe Enough?* ed. Richard C. Schwing and Walter A. Albers, Jr. (New York–London: Plenum Press, 1980).

much to enrich all human life. Consider the rush to "do something" (that is, to impose costs and restrict freedom) about a problem such as the greenhouse effect. This problem, to be charitable, remains quite conjectural and has not attracted a scientific consensus; a rush to action is a rejection of a basic tenet of liberalism. John Stuart Mill put it as follows:

> . . . in practical matters, the burden of proof is supposed to be with those who are against . . . any limitation of the general freedom of human action. . . . The *a priori* presumption is in favor of freedom and impartiality.[5]

Aaron Wildavsky has pointed out, correctly, that most technologies have not been understood in theory but rather have advanced by a process of trial and error, or by what economists call learning by doing.[6] Yet our society increasingly demands trial without error: it refuses to allow a new technology to be tried until assurances can be given that the technology is completely safe. But such assurances cannot, in general, be given. Without trial and error, no new knowledge will be generated and no further economic progress achieved. Yet economic progress is precisely what has produced a society that is significantly safer than it was, say, 100 years ago: life expectancy and economic growth are highly correlated. The paradox is that a world without economic growth and with no errors would probably be less safe (in terms of life expectancy) in 20–50 years than a world with growth and errors along the way. Wildavsky, for example, presents estimates which indicate that a 15 percent increase in income for the typical British middle-aged manufacturing worker in the 1970s would have had about the same risk-reducing effects as eliminating *all* known hazards from the workplace.[7]

The attitudes of the American people concerning environmental and health risks are so convoluted that they defy the understanding of social scientists. People seem to have only marginal concern over costs, but rather appear to have vague feelings of dread, worry,

[5]John Stuart Mill, *The Subjection of Women* (Buffalo: Prometheus Books, 1986), p. 8.

[6]Aaron Wildavsky, *Searching for Safety* (New Brunswick, N.J.: Transaction Books, 1988).

[7]Ibid., p. 63.

and fear of newness.[8] Paul Slovic, an eminent scholar of decision-making, notes great anomalies between how members of groups such as the League of Women Voters rank certain risky activities and the ratings given to the same activities by experts. Of 30 activities and technologies, ranging from motor vehicles to nuclear power, Slovic notes that both women voters and college students rank nuclear power as the most dangerous while the experts rate it 20th, far behind motor vehicles, smoking, and alcoholic beverages (see Table 1).[9] One difference seems to be that experts view risk in terms of actual mortality, whereas those respondents seem to think about such factors as lack of control, general dread, and catastrophic potential. Slovic has mused that discussions with people about such risks may not really be about risk at all, but rather about some other hidden agenda.

Emotional feelings about risks to health and the environment did not arise in a vacuum. We have built a government bureaucracy and a set of private environmental advocacy institutions designed to expose environmental and health risks, and we should not be surprised at their self-interested zeal in doing so. Studies by organizations such as the Media Institute have shown that reporting on environmental issues tends to rely heavily on government sources and much less on industry or independent sources.[10] Further, since government sources are prone to assess a higher degree of risk in any given environmental incident than are industry or independent spokespersons, the stories are slanted in an alarmist direction.

In addition, the private environmental movement has become expert in the use and manipulation of the press. For example, public-relations specialist David Fenton of Fenton Communications, who manufactured the Alar scare for the Natural Resources Defense Council, bragged about the tremendous media exposure

[8]See Richard T. Carson and John K. Horowitz, "The Many Facets of Health Risks: Valuing the Characteristics." (Paper presented before the American Economic Association, Atlanta, December 1989.)

[9]Paul Slovic, "Perception of Risk," *Science*, April 17, 1987, pp. 280–85.

[10]The Media Institute, *Chemical Risks: Facts, Fears, and the Media* (Washington: The Media Institute, 1985); also Peter M. Sandman et al., *Environmental Risk and the Press*, (New Brunswick, N.J.: Transaction Books, 1987).

Table 1.
ORDERING OF RISK BY THREE GROUPS.
(RANK 1 IS MOST RISKY.)

Activity or Technology	League of Women Voters	College Students	Experts
Nuclear power	1	1	20
Motor vehicles	2	5	1
Handguns	3	2	4
Smoking	4	3	2
Motorcycles	5	6	6
Alcoholic beverages	6	7	3
Private aviation	7	15	12
Police work	8	8	17
Pesticides	9	4	8
Surgery	10	11	5
Fire fighting	11	10	18
Large construction	12	14	13
Hunting	13	18	23
Spray cans	14	13	26
Mountain climbing	15	22	29
Bicycles	16	24	15
Commercial aviation	17	16	16
Electric power (nonnuclear)	18	19	9
Swimming	19	30	10
Contraceptives	20	9	11
Skiing	21	25	30
X-rays	22	17	7
High school and college football	23	26	27
Railroads	24	23	19
Food preservatives	25	12	14
Food coloring	26	20	21
Power mowers	27	28	28
Prescription antibiotics	28	21	24
Home appliances	29	27	22
Vaccinations	30	29	25

SOURCE: Paul Slovic, "Perception of Risks," *Science*, April 17, 1987, p. 281.

for NRDC that was obtained for a small investment.[11] Liberal segments of the press have been most accommodating in spreading the gospel that insensitive ("Big") business is the major cause of our environmental problems. Again, Eric Hoffer had it right: "Mass movements can rise and spread without a belief in God, but never without belief in a devil."[12]

The power of the media to distort an environmental story is classically illustrated with the incident at Love Canal. Almost every environmentally informed American has a vague memory that at Love Canal some chemical company or the other poisoned a lot of people with a hazardous waste dump. What is almost impossible to find in the press accounts is the fact that a perfectly safe disposal area, formerly owned by Hooker Chemical, was disturbed by an arm of the Niagara Falls city government over the almost constant protest of Hooker Chemical. Hooker was convicted by the press, and Superfund (originally a $9.2 billion federal cleanup fund for hazardous wastes) was born. Since that time (the late 1970s) there has never been any generally accepted scientific evidence of harm to anyone living in the area.[13] As of August 1990, part of the previously condemned residential area at Love Canal was allowed to reopen, and 10 houses in the area were scheduled to go on sale. There were hundreds of applicants for those houses. However, the Sierra Club and NRDC announced plans to fight the sale in court. Love Canal was and still is a media event: it allowed the environmental movement to extend its influence from the air and water to the land itself.

Love Canal not only had the effect of generating Superfund, thousands of regulations for the chemical industry, and higher chemical prices all around, but it also helped to give rise to the NIMBY (not in my back yard) effect for disposal sites of all kinds. People have become so fearful of disposal sites that they will not

[11]David Brooks, "Saving the Earth from Its Friends," *National Review*, April 1, 1990, pp. 28–31.

[12]Hoffer, p. 89.

[13]See Richard L. Stroup and Jane S. Shaw, "The Free Market and the Environment," *Public Interest*, Fall 1989, pp. 30–43. One of us (Bolch) was working on a hazardous waste research team at Vanderbilt University at the time of Love Canal. He was never successful in finding a member of the press who would write the full story of that celebrated "environmental disaster."

allow them at all. The media now point to garbage barges floating in the Atlantic and warn that we are in serious trouble because existing disposal sites are filling up. Of course, existing sites are filling up. The problem is that new sites are not being opened. In fact, in April 1990, a major player in the hazardous waste disposal business, Browning-Ferris, took a $295 million after-tax write-off and, citing difficulties with permitting, left the hazardous waste business altogether.[14]

The Anthropomorphism of Nature

The lack of rationality over the environment is well illustrated by the radical proposals of people such as Roderick Nash in his book *The Rights of Nature*.[15] Nash held that the rights of human beings should no longer be taken as superior to those of nature. And in recent years, advocates such as Christopher D. Stone and Laurence H. Tribe have wondered about representing nature in courts of law.[16] Supporters of granting nature the ethical and legal status of human beings display a chutzpah that is difficult to comprehend, because they imply that, like some mad priest with a fancied pipeline to God, they know what nature wants. To paraphrase environmental commentator Mark Sagoff, how can one know that the empty mountain over there does not *want* to become a ski resort? Could strip mining be pleasurable to nature? One can have a lot of fun asking such absurd questions.

The anthropomorphism of nature has a long and frightening history in the environmental movement, the roots of which are traced in an excellent book by Anna Bramwell, *Ecology in the 20th Century: A History*.[17] Bramwell points out that "ecologism" grew up in the 19th century, having a lineage in both holistic biology and energy economics. Ecologism took firm root in Germany where it became a major element of the Third Reich, the first government,

---

[14]As reported in their "Second Quarter Report," 1990.

[15]Roderick Nash, *The Rights of Nature* (Madison: University of Wisconsin Press, 1989).

[16]See Joel Schwartz, "The Rights of Nature and the Death of God," *Public Interest*, Fall 1989, pp. 3–13.

[17]Anna Bramwell, *Ecology in the 20th Century: A History* (New Haven, Conn.: Yale University Press, 1989).

according to Bramwell, to be dominated by radical environmentalists. The oak leaf as symbol of the Nazi SS, the motto of "Blood and Soil," the possible need to sacrifice mankind to nature, the fixation with tree planting, the state control of natural resources, and many other familiar ecological themes were present in Hitler's Germany.

After the war the Greens moved from right to left, a change unsurprising to people who accept F. A. Hayek's contention that all totalitarian systems are in reality the same. The Green movement has embraced nomadic bands of witches, anti-nuclear activists, Celtic nationalists, sun worshipers, and discontented persons of all stripes. Technology is generally damned but is more acceptable if it is small or rural. Trade is considered to be a symptom of lack of balance, and the market mechanism is rejected as a form of slavery. As Bramwell documents, the radical Green movement advocates self-sufficient, often communal, economic zones that would be prohibited from exchanging goods with other zones.[18]

Bramwell correctly identifies ecologism with a death wish: a very large fraction of the five billion or so persons on earth simply cannot survive without the technology and trade that exist today. A world run by radical Greens would result in a mass extermination of human beings that would make the combined performances of Hitler, Stalin, and Mao pale by comparison.

The Greens are now a dominant political force in Europe. Both there and in the United States, Green has replaced Red as the symbol of the political Left: at a recent meeting on the future of the Left held in Colorado, the discussion quickly turned to toxic waste, nuclear power, and other Green issues.[19]

Green Power, Green Politics

The National Wildlife Federation claims almost six million members, and Greenpeace's membership exceeds two million. The total annual budgets of U.S. environmental advocacy groups alone are estimated to exceed a quarter of a billion dollars.[20] With that kind of power and money at stake, no wonder new "threats" to mankind

---

[18]Ibid., pp. 92–93, 102–3, 152.

[19]As reported in the *Economist*, April 21, 1990, p. 31.

[20]As reported by Warren T. Brookes, "The Green Network Grows Greener with Cash," *Human Events*, May 19, 1990, p. 414.

and the environment are discovered almost daily. The political strategy is disarmingly simple: keep the movement in the public eye by demanding (and then railing when not getting) the impossible (zero pollution), while continuously canvassing the scientific community for new issues. Scientists, especially academic scientists, are easily flattered with cocktail parties and press conferences, and can be counted on for a steady stream of new ideas. But even if no completely new problems are discovered, advancing techniques of scientific measurement guarantee that smaller and smaller levels of problem substances can be identified in an increasing number of things, such as polar ice or mother's milk.

Meanwhile, none of this power or money is ignored by the politicians who quickly learn how to manipulate environmental issues to their own benefit. When a new law is written, the as-yet-unbuilt production facility is generally regulated to a greater degree than the grandfathered existing facilities. Why? Because the unbuilt facility has no vote. Industry accepts that kind of legislation because it provides a future barrier to competition, but the American people lose both environmentally and economically because technology is locked in. For example, as a result of regulatory disincentives to build new plants, U.S. electric generating facilities are rapidly aging: in 1970 only 2 percent of U.S. electric generating capacity was more than 30 years old; it is predicted that by 2000 the average age will be 30 years.[21] The drastic aging of plants in such a vital industry may be rational in the context of short-run political considerations but it is clearly not rational on technological, ecological, or economic grounds. Obviously, aging plants can be expected to be both relatively inefficient in energy usage and more polluting than more modern facilities. What is disturbing is that political rationality may be, as Robert Hahn suggests, the only rationality in the environmental movement, given its propensity to ignore science and economics.[22]

Environmental Choice

The American people must understand that waste products are naturally created by any activity (economic or otherwise). Environmental damage can be controlled only by using scarce resources

---

[21]Richard E. Balzhiser and Kurt E. Yeager, "Coal-Fired Power Plants for the Future," *Scientific American*, September 1987, p. 103.

[22]Robert W. Hahn, "The Politics and Religion of Clean Air," *Regulation*, Winter 1990, pp. 21–30.

that might be better used elsewhere. If people have an ethical need to leave their children a better world, it might be quite rational to allow some pollution while spending resources on, say, bridges. The environmental problem is not some moral or ethical absolute but is rather, like most things, an economic and political problem that requires choices. Perhaps the most important thing to understand about the environment is that it has become a metaphor for the trouble this nation is bringing on itself by its refusal to make political and economic choices. Like some aspects of welfare, the environment is increasingly considered to be an entitlement rather than something that must be paid for by sacrifice. When people say that the environment must be protected at all costs, either they are expressing something akin to religious fanaticism, or they feel that the costs will be borne by someone else.

Environmentalism has a checkered history at best, and those who benefit from the environmental movement are surely no more moral than those who tend to be too busy to worry about the environment at all. As Hoffer maintained, environmentalists may simply be bored with their lives. The rhetoric of the first-rate lawyers and the second-rate scientists who pretend to represent nature and the public needs increased scrutiny. Nature is a choice, and both rationality and morality insist that environmentalism not be confused with religion. David Stolinsky put it very well:

> The problem is that religious feelings tend to be associated not only with zeal but also with non-logical thinking. In science as in everyday life, when we try one possible solution, if it does not work we try another. But in religion, we persist in doing what does not work so long as we perceive it as being "good.". . . And it is all too easy to mistake feeling good for doing good. In addition, believing that those who disagree with us are not just mistaken but *wrong*—that is, criminal or sinful—leads to intolerance. Non-logical thinking and contempt for one's opponents are not useful tools for solving problems in a democracy.[23]

---

[23]Letter by David C. Stolinsky, *Commentary*, April 3, 1990, p. 3.

3. The Population Problem: A Revisionist Perspective

A basic theme of the environmental movement is that the growth rate of world population should be slowed or even reversed. It is said that there are simply too many people pressing on a finite resource base. A more moderate claim is that even if there is not excess population now, there soon will be; the need for planned, even coerced, population control is critical for continued existence on this finite spaceship earth.

The argument is so starkly simple that it is taken to be valid by an overwhelming number of people, especially the intellectual classes of the developed world. Yet the idea is flawed at every turn: in its view that there is, or soon will be, excess population; that the resource base of the world is finite in any near-term, economically meaningful sense; or that planning is needed to control population growth rates.

The roots of the excess population theme go back to an economist of the late 18th and early 19th centuries, Thomas Robert Malthus. Malthus believed that passion between the sexes was inevitable and that consequently, population growth was and would continue to be rapid. On the other hand, food production was difficult and slow. In fact, population growth would be geometric, while food production would, at best, grow at an arithmetic rate. Mathematically, no matter how small a starting value is given to population or how large a starting value is given to food, Malthus's assumptions ensure that population will eventually overtake the food supply. Since mankind is unlikely to prevent its clash with the eventual limits of food resources by reining in its collective sexual appetite, no set of simple reforms will check the growth of population. That control will have to come from such things as war, famine, and pestilence. Economics was indeed a "dismal science." (For the record, Malthus "soften[ed] some of the harshest conclusions" when he revised his *Essay on the Principle of Population*.)

Impressed by Malthus's reasoning, Charles Darwin borrowed the concept of the struggle of man against the limits of resources and applied it to all living organisms. Karl Marx, in turn, appropriated Darwin's evolutionary thinking to form a key part of his own theory of the progression of society along lines set down by natural history.[1] The environmental movement would subsequently amend Malthus's metaphor of "food" to include all resources, many of which seemingly had no growth rate at all, and scientists would distinguish between "renewable" and "exhaustible" resources.

Population and Economic Growth

Today most economists treat Malthus as an interesting example of how wrong you can be if you fail to understand the driving force of economic progress—technological change. Global food production has more than kept pace with population growth, and the food surpluses have caused severe political and economic problems in many nations, including the United States. For those countries where famine remains a problem, the cause is usually not a global failure of production but rather a failure in distribution. When local production is insufficient, the cause can often be traced to price controls, trade restrictions, or collective farming, all of which discourage output, or to political groups that use food as a weapon against their own people. Globally, food is simply not a limiting factor to population growth for the foreseeable future.[2]

If Malthus thought that population was excessive in his day, surely it must be a problem by now. Just how many people are there on the earth? To say there are around five billion means very little to most people. Instead, that number can be put in perspective by asking what would happen if the world's people were put into the land area of Texas: each person would have an area equal to the floor space of a typical U.S. home.[3] Indeed, some cities in the

[1]See Henryk Grossman, "The Evolutionist Revolt against Classical Economics," in *Essays in Economic Thought: Aristotle to Marshall*, ed. Joseph J. Spengler and William R. Allen (Chicago: Rand McNally, 1960).

[2]See, for example, Roger Revelle, "The World Supply of Agricultural Land," in *The Resourceful Earth: A Response to Global 2000*, ed. Julian Simon and Herman Kahn (Oxford: Blackwell, 1984).

[3]The *World Almanac* for 1990 lists the world population at 5.192 billion persons and the square land miles of Texas at 262,017. Simple arithmetic shows each person placed in Texas would have about 1,400 square feet.

United States, such as Jacksonville, Florida, contain enough land area to provide standing room for the entire global population.[4]

Anyone who has looked out an airplane window while traveling across this country knows how empty the United States really is. High population densities are usually associated with Asian countries. In fact, Japan, India, and China all have population densities (persons per square mile) lower than that of New Jersey, and the population density of China is less than that of either Switzerland or Denmark and half that of West Germany. Even India is only slightly more densely populated than West Germany, and the United States, by comparison, has hardly any population at all.[5] That many Asian cities are teeming with people has as much to do with private and public choices (such as subsidies that aid urban dwellers at the expense of farmers) as with any physical shortage of real estate.

There is, of course, no way to refute a forecast until the time for the forecasted activity comes to pass. Yet population (like weather) forecasting is a very uncertain occupation.[6] It does seem fairly clear, however, that countries achieving a high level of economic development seem to have a natural propensity to slow their population growth. For the United States, not only has the rate of growth fallen substantially in the past decade, but the rate of growth in number of children under age five is now approaching negative levels. Similar growth changes can be cited for Canada, Western Europe, Australia, Japan, Hong Kong, and Singapore. For some of those places the population problem in the foreseeable future is likely to be too slow a rate of growth. The impending Social Security problem and young-worker shortage are two widely recognized manifestations of the problem in the United States.

In the less developed world, the tendency toward large families may be driven not so much by Malthusian lust as by a desire for

[4]The land area of this city is 776 square miles, enough to provide a little over 4 square feet of space for each person in the world.

[5]The following are population densities in persons per square mile: Japan, 844; New Jersey, 1,034; Switzerland, 406; Denmark, 305; West Germany, 626; China, 288; India, 658; United States, 68. *World Almanac* (1990).

[6]Even in the United States where data, experts, and computation facilities abound, the fall in fertility in the 1960s took experts completely by surprise. See Landon Y. Jones, *Great Expectations: America and the Baby Boom Generation* (New York: Coward, McCann, and Geoghegan, 1980).

social security. At low levels of economic development, the force of mortality is so great that if a husband and wife wish to ensure that they will have children to care for them in old age, the only prudent thing to do is to have a large number of children. Birth control methods are known in all parts of the world and have been practiced throughout recorded history. Large families are often produced not out of ignorance but out of reasoned choice. Paradoxically, one way to cause the growth rate of population to slow in the long run (but not the short) may be to follow economic policies that are associated with a reduction in the mortality rate: the creation of institutions that will allow sustained economic growth, something that is almost always accompanied by improvements in both private health care and public health facilities. Two principal reasons why population rates have slowed toward zero or even negative levels in much of the industrialized world are first, the relative security that higher levels of income and wealth provide, and second, the increased freedom for women that generally accompanies economic growth. By promoting ecologically driven policies that seek to limit economic growth, the environmental movement may be ensuring the defeat of one of its basic aspirations.

The concern over population growth in the less developed nations was given added significance several decades ago because of massive research and development funding by the Rockefeller and Ford foundations. Originally, the fear was that high levels of population growth would prevent economic development. But empirically, there seems to be no significant correlation between either population densities or population growth rates and income per capita among the nations of the world.[7] While it is now not particularly controversial to argue that high levels of income can lead to reduced population growth, it is not at all clear that high population growth rates either speed or retard economic development. The problem is in which direction to point the causal arrow: economic development to population, or the reverse. Many European nations experienced high rates of population growth during their most rapid periods of development, but others, such as India

[7]There is some indication that higher population density stimulates economic growth for less developed countries, but the data for more developed countries have yet to show any association between density and growth. See Julian Simon, *Theory of Population and Economic Growth* (Oxford: Blackwell, 1986), pp. 64–65.

and China, have experienced high population growth rates during periods of economic decline. Some countries with relatively high population densities (such as Japan, Hong Kong, and Singapore) are relatively rich while other, low-density countries (such as Ethiopia, Uganda, and Zaire) remain relatively poor. Stranger yet, there is no consistent difference in the natural resource bases of countries that can explain their differing economic circumstances.

Nevertheless, does common sense not dictate that reduction in population can bring relief for the desperate economic conditions of the most impoverished nations? It is said that there are two ways to increase output per capita in the short run: increase output with the same population or reduce population with the same output. Economist Stephen Enke pointed out that since children do not produce but only consume for the first few years of their lives, they are a net burden to the economy in the short run. That burden is offset only later when the child has grown to adulthood and begins producing.[8] The question is whether the short-run burden will be offset by enough later production to create a lifetime net benefit to society.

The proper calculation, says Enke, is the common business practice of discounting, which uses a rate of interest to adjust the near-term loss and the far-term gains to a common time dimension. Discounting recognizes that a dollar of returns tomorrow is worth less than a dollar of returns today because waiting is involved. In the mathematics of discounting, the higher the interest rate, the less valuable is a dollar of future returns relative to a dollar of present returns. People who discount with high interest rates are less willing to wait for returns than those who discount with low interest rates.

Clearly, for a high enough interest rate, the burden of present consumption for a child will never be offset by the child's future production because great weight will be put on the near-term losses relative to the far-term gains. Thus, says Enke, society may be able to increase output per capita in the short run at a net saving to itself by investing in simple birth control devices, such as IUDs or condoms.

---

[8]Stephen Enke,"The Economic Aspects of Slowing Population Growth," *Economic Journal,* March 1966, pp. 44–56.

We may grant that this argument is correct in the short run but only for a relatively small number of prevented births. It cannot be true if the births of a large number of children are prevented; in the extreme case of the prevention of all childbirths, the economy will necessarily move to a position of no population at all: it will have committed demographic suicide. Clearly, some optimum number of prevented births is called for, but we have no method of calculation that will tell us what that optimum is. Quite obviously, the calculated benefit that can be obtained from a prevented birth depends on the determination of a social interest rate, a concept that economists have never been able to quantify. If one chooses a relatively high social interest rate, then early consumption will definitely outweigh later production in most plausible situations: a high social interest rate implies that great weight is given to the near-term consumption effect, and little weight to the far-term production effect. Yet, to the extent that those who would prevent births because of a calculation based on a high social interest rate are the same persons who insist on conservation of resources for future generations, there is a rudimentary conflict. If the birth controllers calculate with high interest rates, the preservationists must calculate with low interest rates to give the distant ecological future great relative importance. The observable fact that these two groups of people are often the same tends to confuse those of us who seek to understand their motives.

Consistency aside, there is by now such a large body of foundation employees, international bureaucrats, health workers, concerned do-gooders, environmentalists, and plain bigots that it is difficult to suggest that perhaps the population problem in the less developed world may not be as serious an impediment to economic growth as some would have us believe. The fanatical belief in the evils of overpopulation is so great in the academic world that the editor of the venerable *Journal of the American Statistical Association* was apparently moved to commission reviews pro and con of a recent book that mildly questioned whether population was a problem for economic development.[9]

[9]See the back-to-back reviews by Nathan Keyfitz and Andrea Tyree of National Research Council, Committee on Population, *Population Growth and Economic Development: Policy Questions* (Washington: National Academy Press, 1986) in the *Journal of the American Statistical Association*, December 1987, pp. 1179–80.

Perhaps the most important lesson to be learned from the question of population control and economic development is that our knowledge of the process of demographic change is meager at best. Theories that are often contradictory have a way of coexisting, and massive demographic changes that are completely unexpected may occur. There is, in this field, a great deal of hand waving.

Population and Resources

In recent years the rhetoric of the population controllers has shifted away from economic development toward a more sinister tale of doomsday. Paul Ehrlich, the Stanford biologist and author of several best-selling books on the terrors of population growth, predicted in the late 1960s that the decades of the 1970s and 1980s would see world hunger, a reduction of life expectancy to 42 years, the death of the ocean, the birth of a Midwestern desert, and other such calamities that never were.[10] In the early 1970s, the highly touted study by Donella Meadows et al. for the Club of Rome, *The Limits to Growth*,[11] predicted the absolute exhaustion of gold by 1981, mercury and silver by 1985, tin by 1987, and petroleum by 1982. Nicholas Georgescu-Roegen produced an erudite book, *The Entropy Law and the Economic Process*, in the early 1970s. The book argued that increasing entropy would, in and of itself, ensure that cheap and available resources would become harder to extract and that markets themselves were suspect in their capability of allocating resources across generations. It was as if, he argued in seminars, God had given mankind a finite bottle of ink with which to write checks. Georgescu-Roegen's book pressed the boundaries of long-run thinking by contemplating matters such as the demise of the universe itself.

Those studies and others were qualitatively different from most of the neo-Malthusian writing that had gone before—they were speaking not of periodic troubles but of absolute exhaustion, a decimation of the planet, a condition of no return. The finite planet earth was viewed as if in a photograph taken from the moon: it was being eaten away by man and excreted into a massive, high-entropy dungheap.

[10]Paul Ehrlich, "Eco-Catastrophe!" *Ramparts*, September 1969, pp. 24–27.

[11]Donella H. Meadows et al., *The Limits to Growth: A Report for the Club of Rome's Project on the Predicament of Mankind* (New York: Universe Books, 1972).

The opposing voices were, and still are, few. While they are often eloquent, those voices are largely ignored by the intellectual community and the press. Julian Simon's brilliant book, *The Ultimate Resource*, echoed a theme that had been developed years before by Simon Kuznets, a Nobel laureate in economics:

> But the scarcity of natural resources in underdeveloped countries is primarily a function of underdevelopment; underdevelopment is not a function of scarce natural resources. . . . Many underdeveloped countries are unaware of their wealth of natural resources since such knowledge is itself a function of economic development.[12]

For Simon Kuznets, like Julian Simon, the ultimate resource was the human mind.

A small but growing group of Western intellectuals called the "population revisionists" has begun to question the entire notion that population is excessive, that resources are pressed by population, or that population needs to be managed. Economist Jacqueline Kasun's recent book, *The War against Population*, explored the ideology and politics of the anti-population crowd in ways that surprised even the specialists in the field.[13] As Julian Simon noted in the preface, that book took great courage to write. It should be read by anyone interested in the population question.

Yet the question remains about the ability of a market-oriented economy to allocate resources across generations. Can resources be allocated across time fairly, or does the "mindless" market mechanism rob our distant heirs of their just share of the finite resource pie? That question, of course, cannot be answered except by historical analogy. If the market does not allocate resources in some equitable way across generations, what process can? The population controllers qua environmentalists answer that people with superior vision should be placed in charge, but no such superior body of councilors seems to have ever been located. We do, however, have some information that is suggestive.

[12]Simon Kuznets, "Population and Economic Growth," *Proceedings of the American Philosophical Society*, June 22, 1967, pp. 170–93.

[13]Jacqueline Kasun, *The War against Population: The Economics and Ideology of Population Control* (San Francisco: Ignatius Press, 1988).

First, it seems clear that some of the greatest environmental disasters of modern times have been experienced in nations with planned economies. Contemporary visitors to Eastern bloc nations are sickened by the environmental damage there. In Poland, for example, lead contamination in the soil is so great in some areas that the government dictated, until faced with a minor revolt, that vegetables should not be grown.

Second, if planning is important, how far ahead should we look? It surely is not clear that we should attempt, as did the Third Reich, to plan for a thousand years, much less a hundred, given the present state of our ability to forecast the future. Indeed, economic history teaches us that it is almost certain that such planning would lock us into a pattern of resource use that would guarantee the exhaustion of the very resources on which we had bet the future. As economists William Baumol and Wallace Oates have pointed out:

> Contrary to what some socialist theorists have suggested, a central lesson of the Soviet experience is that governmental ownership and central planning do not automatically do away with the abuse of society's natural resources and its quality of life. . . . This reminder is important for us because we are apt to forget that, even in a free market economy, government activities produce quite a significant share of environmental damage.[14]

Third, the preservation of aesthetic resources (such as pleasing vistas) is, apart from hunter-gatherer societies, a game that only the rich can afford to play. If the troubles of Soviet-style economies have anything to teach us, it is that such economies are not able to generate a level of income and wealth comparable to market-oriented economies. In the United States of 100 years ago, when the level of economic development was probably on a par with what is to be found in Egypt today, captains of industry proudly commissioned portraits of themselves framed against a background of smokestacks—the resource of a blue sky had yet to be discovered.

It is precisely the refusal of the finite resource school to rely on the market economy that has made its predictions so egregiously

[14]William J. Baumol and Wallace E. Oates, *Economics, Environmental Policy, and the Quality of Life* (Englewood Cliffs, N.J.: Prentice-Hall, 1979), pp. 80–81.

false in recent years. As another Nobel laureate in economics, F. A. Hayek, has made clear, a market system is able to impart information, in the form of prices, on which resources are relatively scarce—information that is without peer in any planned system. Because people are not fools, when a given resource becomes scarce relative to a plausible substitute, they will shift away from the relatively scarce resource and toward the substitute. Predictions based on mere physical quantities and not on the dynamic evolution of relative prices is destined to failure in a market economy. This neglect of relative prices was the basic problem with the forecasts of the Club of Rome and continues to be the difficulty with all other such forecasts based on physical quantities and prepared with an engineer's mentality. The interesting part of studying resources is not that they are in some physical sense finite but that their changing relative prices avert the physical exhaustion that would otherwise come to pass.

Economic history is so replete with examples of shifts away from relatively expensive resources toward relatively inexpensive ones that for most people only a gentle nudge is needed to bring a flood of examples to mind. Even more astonishing is that those shifts often took place in ways that were totally unexpected by the most brilliant minds of the day. Just as the most gifted attorney is never able to predict all the twists and turns of a court case, so the ability of a planner to contemplate the permutations of a given physical resource difficulty is limited in the extreme.

A favorite story among economic historians is the case of England before the Industrial Revolution when a basic resource, wood, was being rapidly depleted. According to John Nef, the eminent economic historian, the price of firewood began to rise at a pace far outstripping the general price level as the physical shortage began to manifest itself in the 16th and 17th centuries.[15] The result was twofold: wood was conserved, and the supply of fuel was enhanced beyond measure as the economy shifted to coal. The use of the steam engine became commonplace because of the need to pump water from coal mines. As an unexpected spin-off, the age of rapid and inexpensive transportation was born. An energy and building material crisis led to the Industrial Revolution. Any conservationist

---

[15]John Nef, *The Rise of the British Coal Industry* (London: Routledge, 1932).

of the day who pointed with alarm to a clear trend in wood depletion would have been sorely mistaken. Were planners able to hold down rising wood prices by rationing or some other means, wood almost surely would have been exhausted, and today's standard of living and greatly enhanced life expectancy might have never come to pass.

But surely the parable of wood in England is ancient history. Does the world not move at a much faster pace today, and will resources, being overburdened by a much larger population, not become depleted before substitutes can be invented? Surely we cannot rely on a technological fix to save us. What about the increased toll of pollution?

In the first place, there has been no upward trend in the relative prices of most natural resources in this century, perhaps because the world is moving so fast that substitutes are constantly being invented to offset any physical depletion in basic resources. Even petroleum—a resource that only 15 years ago was widely predicted to skyrocket in price as it neared exhaustion—has fallen drastically in relative price (except during periods of "political shortage" such as the Iraq episode). Now rather than hearing dire warnings about petroleum, we are treated to PBS broadcasts which declare that the world is full of oil. Perhaps, as Julian Simon has suggested, the things viewed as basic resources are desired for rather simple reasons such as hardness or conductivity—properties that are relatively amenable to substitution, given the powers of science.

A current example of the shift from a relatively scarce resource (copper) toward one less scarce (sand) is taking place at this very moment as communications companies move to replace copper wires with "wires" made of glass. The steady fall in copper prices relative to either wages or consumer prices has been documented by Julian Simon, as have similar trends in the relative prices of pig iron, pig lead, aluminum, agricultural land, and many other natural resources.[16]

Second, by almost any standard, the environments of the Western industrialized nations are cleaner today than they have been at almost any time this century. No longer do major cities need to

---

[16]Julian Simon, *The Ultimate Resource* (Princeton, N.J.: Princeton University Press, 1981).

turn on street lights during winter days to compensate for the darkness of pollution created by coal. And surely the best single index of environmental quality is life expectancy, something that has been increasing markedly in market-oriented countries.

If it cannot be shown in any convincing way either that resources are near exhaustion or that the environment is deteriorating, the case for reducing population seems to hinge either on predictions that the future will be worse than the past or on moral concerns.

Predictions and Morals

The record of predictions about population is too poor to generate much confidence that the current predictions of doom are any better than those of the past. Malthus was wrong nearly 200 years ago, and the odds are great that neo-Malthusians are wrong today. There is every indication that economic development itself acts as a brake on population growth. Therefore, if poor nations are allowed to develop, a reduction in their population growth is at least as likely as continued population growth. (Recent articles in business journals such as *Fortune* predict an impending worldwide labor shortage, underscoring the fact that one truly scarce resource continues to be people.[17])

The moral issue is quite simply stated: Is the growth of population, or its absolute size, morally wrong? If so, why? (Toward the end of a lengthy review of the population question, economist Allen Kelly fell back on the moral issue after finding that "there is no believable and generally accepted quantitative estimate of population's impact on development."[18])

Everyone has a set of moral attitudes about population growth and a set of motivations (ranging from the purely selfish to the sublimely munificent) that is entangled with those moral beliefs. The question is, should people impose their moral views on others?

Many people who worry about population clearly aspire to impose controls on others—and make a living doing so. But no branch of science or economics can tell us what the proper rate of population growth should be. Indeed, history offers the suggestion

[17]Louis S. Richman, "The Coming World Labor Shortage," *Fortune*, April 9, 1990, pp. 69–77.

[18]Allen Kelly, "The Economic Consequences of Population Change in the Third World," *Journal of Economic Literature*, December 1988, p. 1715.

that moral considerations concerning population may well backfire in ways that are altogether immoral. One of the reasons why Jacqueline Kasun's recent book took courage to publish is that she frankly treats a issue that students of population have generally sidestepped: What is the role of eugenics in this debate? Why do population controllers feel that they have the answer to the question: Who is, and is not, fit to reproduce? To live?

The not-so-distant experience of Jews and other "unworthy" minority groups with the fruits of eugenic thinking clearly reinforces the case that population matters are better left alone, rather than turned over to the "best" minds in society. In contemplating these issues, people should ask themselves, as have sociologists Milton Himmelfarb and Victor Baras, on which groups do they want to impose zero population growth?[19] And why are those groups generally not ones to which they belong? Nagging doubts about the answers to those questions should touch their hearts even if the economic and scientific arguments given here fail to touch their intellects.

[19]Milton Himmelfarb and Victor Baras, *Zero Population Growth: For Whom?* (Westport, Conn.: Greenwood Press, 1975).

4. Chemophobia in America

On February 28, 1978, Russell E. Train, then administrator of the Environmental Protection Agency, declared to an audience of news people at the National Press Club in Washington, D.C., that because of the toxic chemicals used in industry, "All America lives in peril." His announcement set the stage for a growing public hysteria that has been aided and abetted by the media, the government, and the growing number of private groups that have declared themselves to be opponents of cancer, birth defects and other things evil. This hysteria has wasted billions of taxpayers' dollars, has no doubt slowed the growth and competitiveness of the economy, and has caused thousands of people to live in fear.

Alar

We begin with the Alar scare, which is almost completely a child of the electronic and print media. The coverage of this "story" was professionally orchestrated by the Fenton Communications Company, which had been retained for this purpose by the Natural Resources Defense Council (NRDC), an activist organization noted more for the excellence of its lawyers than for the quality of its science.

The campaign was inaugurated in February 1989 with a segment on the television program "Sixty Minutes" in which the public was informed of a carcinogenic hazard presented by apples treated with the chemical Alar. Close on the heels of this national media exposure came actress Meryl Streep, who apparently was looking for a worthy cause to enhance her image. On March 7 Streep announced the formation of Mothers and Others for Pesticide Limits. Coverage of this event was provided by, among others, *USA Today* and the television shows "Today" and "Phil Donahue." In all of these presentations, any scientific evidence that Alar was not a significant health risk was generally dismissed as being offered by "lackeys" of the chemical or the apple industry. The interviews on "Sixty

Minutes," for example, have been characterized as a "public inquisition"[1] by Ernest Volkmann, a long-time observer of the chemical industry and retired chemical engineer. Even though the apple industry had known of the pending NRDC report for over a year, the industry reportedly was completely taken aback by the slickness and effectiveness of the media blitz.[2]

What is Alar and how dangerous is it? Alar is Uniroyal's trade name for a water-soluble crystalline material whose scientific name is 2,2-dimethylhydrazide. Also known as daminozide, it slowly decomposes to form small amounts of UDMH (unsymmetrical dimethylhydrazine). Alar acts as a growth regulator and delays ripening of apples to prevent them from dropping from trees prematurely. It also delays ripening in storage and thus is valuable in ensuring that apples will be more abundant for more of the year than otherwise. Alar not only reduces the cost of apples but, as we shall see, it also may be good for the environment. That benefit was generally overlooked in the media coverage, which noted only that the breakdown product of Alar, UDMH, had been found to be carcinogenic when fed in massive doses to rodents.

Although earlier studies by the Food and Drug Research Laboratories had found Alar to be noncarcinogenic, in 1977 Bela Toth of the Eppley Institute announced tests that were claimed to show that Alar presented a serious cancer risk and that its use on food crops should be banned.[3]

EPA decisions to ban chemicals are reviewed by a group of distinguished scientists nominated by the National Science Foundation and the National Institutes of Health. That group, known as the Scientific Advisory Panel, reviewed the Toth data and found them to be so seriously flawed that the results were judged to be invalid. Among other things, the dose given the experimental animals was equivalent to a human's consuming 50,000 pounds of Alar-treated apples per day for a lifetime, controls were not properly examined, and the animals that received Alar were apparently in a state of

[1]Ernest W. Volkmann, "Alar Controversy," *Chemical and Engineering News*, December 4, 1989, pp. 2–3.

[2]Alan R. Newman, "The Great Fruit Scares of 1989," *Analytical Chemistry*, July 15, 1989, pp. 861–63.

[3]Ralph I. Freudenthal and Susan L. Freudenthal, *What You Need to Know to Live with Chemicals* (Green Hills Farms, Conn.: Hill and Garnett, 1989).

dehydration.[4] The NRDC nevertheless used the rejected data in its anti-Alar campaign.

To maintain the registration of Alar, Uniroyal was asked by EPA early in the 1980s to conduct new cancer studies. Those studies, conducted by Uniroyal and independent laboratories, continued to show that Alar was not carcinogenic in either rats or mice, but UDMH in massive doses (equivalent to 19,000 quarts of apple juice per day for the life for a human) was implicated in blood vessel tumors in mice.[5]

Bruce Ames, professor of biochemistry at the University of California, Berkeley, is a widely known biochemist who developed the most extensively used scientific test for mutagenic substances. The test is referred to in scientific literature as the Ames Test. Ames is a world-class authority on evaluating carcinogenic hazards from natural and synthetic foods and food additives. In a letter with Lois Gold published in a May 1989 issue of *Science*, Ames attempted to inject a modicum of scientific reason into the Alar controversy. The letter pointed out that 99.99 percent of pesticides are natural and that

> It is probable that almost every plant product in the supermarket contains natural carcinogens . . . [including] anise, apples, bananas, basil, broccoli, Brussels sprouts, cabbage, cantaloupe, carrots, cauliflower, celery, cinnamon, cloves, cocoa, comfrey tea, fennel, grapefruit juice, honeydew melon, horseradish, kale, mushrooms, mustard, nutmeg, orange juice, parsley, parsnips, peaches, black pepper, pineapples, radishes, raspberries, tarragon and turnips.[6]

When given to rodents in large enough doses, a number of other common substances have been linked to cancer or other health problems. For example, a bulky reference compendium edited by Newton Sax and titled *Dangerous Properties of Industrial Materials* lists fructose, lactose, and maltose as suspected carcinogens.[7] Fructose is

[4]Ibid.

[5]Ibid.

[6]Bruce N. Ames and Lois S. Gold, "Pesticides, Risk, and Applesauce," *Science*, May 19, 1989, pp. 755–57.

[7]Newton I. Sax, *Dangerous Properties of Industrial Materials* (New York: Reinhold, 1963).

a principal constituent of honey, lactose is the principal sugar in milk, and maltose is the main ingredient in starch. Even sucrose (table sugar) and sodium chloride (table salt) have been listed as teratogens, or compounds implicated in birth defects.[8] If the condemnation of milk, honey, common salt, and sugar sounds somewhat excessive, then you may wish to contemplate that if the country decided to ban all natural food items with linkages to cancer or birth defects, everyone would all no doubt starve to death in short order.

This long list of common products is not meant to frighten but rather to point out that something is wrong with the scientific assessment of carcinogens: there are simply too many of them to be believed. Fortunately, as Ames and Gold pointed out, our bodies have developed several lines of defense against toxins, defenses that are quite unable to tell whether a given toxin is natural or synthetic. The inability to discriminate between natural and synthetic toxins is important because, given the furor about synthetic pesticides and the lack of excitement over natural carcinogenic pesticides, plant growers are busy breeding crop strains that are naturally resistant to pests. Some of the new strains are so toxic to human beings that in one case (a new type of celery) the plant causes contact dermatitis among produce workers.

The Ames and Gold estimate of the hazard from consuming a 6-ounce glass of apple juice made from Alar-treated apples each day for a lifetime is about equal to that of consuming, each day, one mushroom, one peanut butter sandwich, one portion of cabbage or Brussels sprouts, or the natural alcohol contained in one glass of orange juice. The risk from eating an apple is one-tenth that of drinking a glass of apple juice.

Nevertheless, why risk another possible carcinogen in apples? For one thing, almost every substance is toxic or safe at some dose, and Alar appears to be as safe as most common natural substances at the levels it is likely to be consumed. Second, curtailing the use of Alar means that untreated fruit will be more susceptible to mold toxins such as patulin: such natural toxins may well be worse for humans than any residual Alar-breakdown compound. Third, Alar reduces the cost and improves the quality of a wholesome food

[8]Simon Roman, "Hidden Dangers," *Nature*, November 30, 1989, p. 474.

product, and anything that increases cost diminishes the chances that the product will be affordable, especially for the poor.

A good example of the absolute need for chemicals in food is peanuts: without fungicides, the potent carcinogen aflatoxin grows on stored peanuts; aflatoxin-contaminated peanuts are high on the list of food carcinogens and a prime cause of cancer in less developed countries (principally in Africa) where fungicides cannot be afforded.[9]

Despite these and other objections from highly respected scientists, pressures by an alarmed public and a politically sensitive Congress resulted in the withdrawal of Alar from the U.S. market by its manufacturer. The Alar case is an excellent example of how practically everyone seems to be heard in the media except knowledgeable scientists.

The Alar story also illustrates the folly of attempting to attach numerical values to risks associated with any supposed cause of cancer. For Alar, the estimated risks of cancer differed by a factor of 25 among the "experts," a disparity caused by the increasing ability of analytical chemists to detect smaller and smaller quantities of potentially hazardous substances and the difficulty of interpreting those new data in terms of quantitatively expressed risk factors.[10] The NRDC estimated that 240 out of every million preschool children would eventually develop cancer as a result of Alar; the EPA's estimate was that nine in a million would be affected, a difference of 25-fold—although virtually no hard evidence supports either figure. The basic problem with those two estimates, or with any estimates for that matter, is that there is simply no way to assign a potency factor that states the number of cancers induced by a given dose of Alar or any other perceived carcinogen.

---

[9]For a description of aflatoxin, see *Dorland's Illustrated Medical Dictionary*, 26th ed. (Philadelphia: Sanders, 1985). Bibliographical sources for aflatoxin problems in Africa can be found in Hector Blackhurst, *Africa, Bibliography, 1989* (Manchester and New York: Manchester University Press, 1990). Peanut butter in the United States is carefully inspected for aflatoxin by specially trained federal inspectors. "Natural" peanut butter is given special attention.

[10]See Leslie Roberts, "Alar: The Numbers Game," *Science*, March 17, 1989, p. 1430.

Statistics and Cancer

Anyone who thinks very much about numerical estimates of cancer risk knows as a matter of common sense that science cannot provide such estimates with any precision. Because we do not generally know the cause or causes of cancer, the only way that science has ever established that a given substance is a carcinogen is by detecting some statistical linkage after the fact—by watching people die from cancer after they have ingested, inhaled, or otherwise been exposed to certain substances. The ideal way to conduct such studies is to identify a group of people before they have been exposed to the substance and to follow them through life until disease occurs or fails to occur. Such studies are called prospective (forward looking). Because prospective studies take a number of years to complete, a faster procedure (but more difficult to validate) is to study a group of people after their exposure to some substance. Inferences about the effects of a particular substance can sometimes be made by comparing the health of an exposed group to that of another (control) group that presumably was not exposed to the suspected substance. That type of study is called retrospective (backward looking) and has the difficulty of not affording as tight a set of controls for extraneous factors as do prospective studies.

One or both of those types of epidemiological (statistical) studies have identified a number of suspected carcinogens, many of them natural: tobacco and alcohol are two of the most potent from the statistical point of view. But even here, all statistical studies are open to the valid criticism that by their very nature they can show only association, not causation. Until we know the cause or causes of human cancer, we will never be able to show by statistics or any other means a clear causal linkage between cancer and any given substance because such a linkage would in and of itself be a demonstration of causation.

A prime antecedent of the public's confusion over numerical cancer estimates is the Delaney Amendment, which was passed by a Congress eager to appease a public alarmed by the threat of carcinogens in the environment. The law prohibits the use in processed food of any substance found to be carcinogenic when fed at high levels to rodents or other test animals. That is a zero risk standard, and it has many problems.

Because it is unethical to experiment on human beings, clear prospective studies using human beings are often impossible. The

major substitute for such studies is experimentation using laboratory animals. While most laboratory studies have the advantage of
being prospective, they often use extraordinarily high doses of the
suspected substance (sometimes a million times higher than would
be encountered in nature). One reason for using these "maximum
tolerated doses" is to ensure a quick response from the animals.
The response needs to be rapid because the natural life expectancy
of the laboratory animals is generally fairly short and because the
cost of labor escalates rapidly with time.

Laboratory results not only need to be quick but also "positive":
they need to show tumors. A researcher who can show that some
substance is associated with cancer is much more apt to enhance
his career (further grants, peer recognition, and promotion) than
one who fails to show a cancer association. Obviously, there is
tremendous pressure, especially on the young investigator, to produce positive results.

The connection between the desire to produce positive results
and spurious statistical inference (not to mention out-and-out scientific fraud) is an open secret in the health research community. In
an excellent paper on statistical methods in epidemiology, Alvin
Feinstein of Yale University School of Medicine condemned (as do
all reputable statisticians) the practice of mining data with statistical
techniques such as "Stepwise Regression." That technique virtually
ensures that if enough "variables" (even those that consist only of
random digits) are investigated, some will end up being "significantly" associated with a bad outcome such as cancer or birth
defects.[11] Feinstein noted, for example, that the research that produced the scare that reserpine (a blood pressure medicine) was a
cause of breast cancer was probably conducted in just such a way.
He wondered why the relationship was upheld by two other studies
before it was established to be false. In a similar way, Feinstein
pointed out how those techniques have produced false linkages
between pancreatic cancer and coffee consumption and between
breast cancer and alcohol consumption. Indeed, Feinstein noted
that literally scores of "cause and effect" statistical studies are in
direct conflict with each other.

[11]Alvin R. Feinstein, "Scientific Standards in Epidemiologic Studies of the Menace
of Daily Life," *Science*, December 2, 1988, pp. 1257–63.

A number of other modern environmental scares are based in whole or in part on statistical inference. Indeed, since the techniques of statistical inference are so poorly understood by the general public (as well as a large part of the scientific community), it is probably worthwhile to make some general comments about them.[12]

Statistical inference is often concerned with looking for the unusual. But to ask if something is unusual, one requires some standard by which to judge unusualness. Statistical inference can assist in setting such a standard but nothing more. It does not indicate, for example, where to look for unusual things: that determination must come from the scientific discipline itself.

Probably the easiest way to understand the process of statistical inference is to consider a jury trial. In the United States, a person is brought to trial only after some official has decided that there is sufficient evidence to warrant a trial. When a person goes to trial, it is because a prosecutor believes that the defendant is guilty. The idea of guilt is what a statistician calls the alternative hypothesis: the prosecutor wishes to prove the hypothesis (or assumption) in court.[13]

The American system of justice, however, does not allow the jury to believe that the accused is guilty before the trial begins. The judge carefully instructs the jury to consider the accused innocent until proven beyond reasonable doubt to be guilty. You may never understand how important this instruction is unless you are forced to face a jury trial. But you can get an inkling of its crucial nature if you ponder the alternative instruction: "You, the jury, are to consider the accused guilty until proven innocent." The hypothesis that the jury is instructed to maintain at the start of a trial is called the null hypothesis by statisticians. It is the same as the instruction the judge actually gives the jury.

During the trial, as evidence accumulates against the accused, the individual members of the jury may change their minds (or fail to do so) in favor of guilt. At what point a juror changes his mind

---

[12]A wonderful exposition of the logic of statistical inference is found in Karl Pearson, *The Grammar of Science* (London: Walter Scott, 1892).

[13]The relationship between jury trials and statistical inference is explored in detail in Cliff Huang and Ben Bolch, "Some Stochastic Aspects of Trial by Jury," *Metron*, June 1976, pp. 73–79.

depends critically on how much evidence the individual juror requires to convict the accused. If the charge is a minor infraction that will result in a fine or a scolding by the judge, then the jury will probably not require as much evidence to convict the accused as it might for a capital crime. The same may be said for any number of prejudices of the jurors: an unkempt, "criminal-looking" young man will probably be convicted on less damaging evidence than will a clean-cut lad of respectful demeanor.

Just how much evidence is required to overthrow the hypothesis of innocence is where statistical inference comes into play. Most statistical studies are based on a method of inference that statisticians call "classical": the researcher (juror) is warned that an error can be made in either of two ways: an innocent person can be convicted, or a guilty person set free. Because in science the researcher dreams up the question in the first place (and thus also acts as the prosecutor), classical inference requires that he conduct his investigation under the null hypothesis (that is, the presumption of innocence). That presumption can be overthrown only after an accumulation of evidence so great that it removes any reasonable doubt of guilt. Those rules may strike you as extremely conservative in that they seem to err on the side of allowing dangerous substances on the market. On the contrary, those rules restrain the scientist who plays the role of both prosecutor and juror. The rules mimic our system of court justice and aim at simple fairness.

The researcher must still specify the amount of evidence needed to overthrow the null hypothesis, and that amount is formalized by something called a significance level. The science of statistics allows the researcher to specify a significance level with a statement such as

> I will continue to believe that nothing unusual is going on unless the evidence is so great that it leads to a logical probability of less than 5 percent that I am right in holding this assumption. In that case, the odds are so small that nothing unusual is going on that I will be forced to reject this hypothesis in favor of the hypothesis that something unusual is going on.

Traditionally, when a null hypothesis seems to hold with a probability of less than 5 percent, it is rejected and the difference is said to be "significant" at the 5 percent level.

47

But a 5 percent significance level carries a great risk. Five percent of the time the null hypothesis will be rejected incorrectly. That is, even when a researcher is looking at numbers that differ from each other only by random amounts, if that researcher does 100 repeated statistical tests on the same set of random numbers, 5 of them on average will indicate that significant (unusual) differences are present. The general public rarely recognizes that repeated statistical tests with the same data will detect significant (unusual) results when only randomness is present. Statisticians call such repeated tests "fishing," and they will tell you that if you fish data long enough, you will eventually "catch" something. Or, if you torture a body of data long enough, it will eventually confess.

The "no fishing" rule of classical statistical inference is most often broken by researchers who develop their research question (alternative hypothesis) from the data itself. Suppose you have two groups of people: one group lives in Chicago, the other in St. Louis. Suppose that you believe those groups have been chosen at random from each city (randomness is a must for most statistical inference and is extremely hard to accomplish in practice). The odds are very great that there will be some difference between them. So you may, for example, believe that people from Chicago like windy days more than people from St. Louis, and you may conduct a statistical test of this suspicion. A good scientist operates under the null hypothesis that there is no difference in preference for wind between the two groups. That is a proper statistical test.

On the other hand, you might ask a research assistant to measure everything possible about the two groups and then to conduct a series of statistical tests to see if anything can be found that is different between them. That technique is fishing. If after a few days of work the research assistant does not report some difference between the two groups, you should fire him because with enough measurements random differences among people will practically ensure that some significant difference will be discovered. The assistant may find, for example, that people from Chicago have, on the average, longer great toes. If, in search of scientific fame, you then report to the press that Chicago's environment produces elongated toes, you have violated the no-fishing rule of classical statistical inference.

A scientist who does discover something from the data (and it is hard sometimes not to do so) has the absolute responsibility to take another independent sample to see if the difference still exists. This retesting with a different sample is replication, and statistical findings that cannot be replicated are generally considered to be worthless.

Because random differences are an essential part of life, even significant statistical differences that are found and later replicated should not be accepted until some reason is given for their existence. Every statistical finding requires a story about why the finding may or may not mean anything. To continue our example, suppose that another sample still produces longer than average great toes for Chicagoans. Does this replicated finding lead to a "Chicago Syndrome"? Not if it is pointed out that the Chicago samples were all taken on a basketball court while those for St. Louis happened to come from a nursery school!

The need for a story (or theory) about why significant differences exist brings up the need to control for extraneous variables. As in our example, significant differences between groups can often be explained by failure to account for some other variable or condition that is the real cause of the observed difference. Some of the most colossal blunders in statistical inference have been made in exactly that way. Dozens of modern statistical textbooks tell of the great *Literary Digest* poll of the 1930s that predicted Alf Landon's defeat of Franklin Roosevelt. The magazine polled over two million people (a huge sample by modern political polling standards). The problem was that those people had all been selected from telephone books, and in those days individuals with telephones were mostly well-to-do and disproportionately Republican.

The *Literary Digest* story is told over and over to budding statisticians to drive home how easy it is to fail to control for an important variable. The better statistics textbooks also point out how meaningless a large sample size can be.[14] Indeed, when someone says good inferences can't be made from small samples, that person has generally revealed his ignorance of statistical methods. A well-selected small sample of as few as three or four is often sufficient for statistical control of the quality of an industrial process. Better a good small sample than a shoddy large one like the *Literary Digest's*.

[14]For example, see the account by Gary Smith, *Statistical Reasoning*, 2d ed. (Boston: Allyn and Bacon, 1988).

These points concerning statistical inference were well illustrated by the recent scare over possible carcinogenic effects of electric power and microwaves. There is no doubt whatsoever that the application of electric power in Alcatraz prison has caused sudden death. There is also no doubt that microwaves can harm living creatures: you should refrain from using a microwave oven to dry a cat! But the pertinent question is whether the exposure received in normal living around electric power, appliances, microwave ovens, and the like is of any concern.

Paul Brodeur's three-part article on the subject in the *New Yorker* in 1989, later incorporated into his book, *Currents of Death: Power Lines, Computer Terminals, and the Attempt to Cover Up Their Threat to Your Health*,[15] is about statistical inference and conspiracy. The conspiracy is so great, according to Brodeur, that it involves the governments of the United States, Canada, and the state of Florida; the EPA; the Occupational Safety and Health Administration; the Food and Drug Administration; the American Medical Association; and such companies as IBM and AT&T, not to mention the Army, Navy, Air Force, and the World Health Organization. By Brodeur's telling, it must be the widest known secret ever held.

The story begins with Nancy Wertheimer, whose doctoral work was in psychology, in which some, but not much, training in statistics is routine. In 1974, Wertheimer was studying leukemia in the greater Denver area. She was searching for causes of this terrible disease by driving around residential areas looking for clustering among victims. "I was," she said, "looking for some kind of pattern."[16] She was, a statistician would say, fishing.

What Wertheimer caught on her fishing expedition was a statistically significant association between childhood cancer and the size and arrangement of power lines in the proximity of children's homes.[17] Because of the lack of money, the published Wertheimer study (done in association with Edward Leeper) did not measure

---

[15]Paul Brodeur, "Annals of Radiation," *New Yorker*, June 12, 1989, pp. 61–88, and *Currents of Death: Power Lines, Computer Terminals, and the Attempt to Cover Up Their Threat to Your Health* (New York: Simon and Schuster, 1989).

[16]Brodeur, "Annals of Radiation," p. 51.

[17]See N. W. Wertheimer and E. Leeper, "Electrical Wiring Configurations and Childhood Cancer," *American Journal of Epidemiology*, March 1979, pp. 273–84.

the strength of the electromagnetic fields actually present, but measured only wiring configurations that were converted into a code for further statistical analysis. Still, the presumption arose that some causal relationship existed between electromagnetic fields and cancer.

The Wertheimer-Leeper study has been roundly criticized on a number of grounds, and replication of its findings in other areas of the country have not been encouraging to its thesis. Fulton, Cobb, and Preble, for example, were unable to replicate the findings for childhood leukemia in Rhode Island.[18] On the other hand, Savitz et al. may have reinforced the Wertheimer-Leeper case by using new Denver data.[19] However, the Savitz study itself is guilty of doing repeated hypothesis tests with the same data, and the strong reservations expressed by the authors of the study point to the tentative nature of their statistical findings. One major indication that all is not well is Savitz's finding that the wiring configuration codes better predict cancer than do the actual measured electromagnetic fields.

The major problem with the electromagnetic scare is that, since chemical bonds are not broken by the fields, there is no consensus on why they should cause cancer. Humanity lives in a sea of electromagnetic radiation. The earth itself produces a powerful magnetic field of about 500 milligauss, as contrasted to the 0.1–10.0 milligauss magnetic fields likely to be generated in your home or office. (Were it not for the fact that the magnetic field of the earth generally dominates, compasses would be of little use.) Again, if statistical findings cannot be reinforced by some theory that makes sense of them, they should probably be ignored.

But to us, by far the most damaging evidence against the case for electricity's causing cancer is the informal statistical study going on around us every day. In this century, particularly in the past 50 years, the United States has gone from a country with practically no man-made electricity to one where electricity is ubiquitous. If, as has been suggested by some of the more militant believers in the carcinogenic properties of electric power, 15 percent of childhood

[18]J. P. Fulton et al., "Electrical Wiring Configurations and Childhood Leukemia in Rhode Island," *American Journal of Epidemiology*, March 1980, pp. 292–96.

[19]David A. Savitz et al. "Case-Control Study of Childhood Cancer and Exposure to 60-Hz Magnetic Fields," *American Journal of Epidemiology*, July 1988, pp. 21–38.

cancers are caused by power-line exposure and an additional 15 percent by exposure to appliances, we should have seen an enormous increase in childhood cancer in the past few decades.[20] Of course, we have not seen such an increase.

At the occupational level, it would seem that for every study that implicates electricity in cancer, there is another one that comes to the opposite conclusion.[21] Again, replication is not a strong point in those statistical studies. And while microwaves can certainly cause harm at levels that actually heat tissue, an extensive study of 20,000 U.S. Navy radar (microwave) operators found no adverse health effects at all in comparison to 20,000 personnel with minimal microwave exposure.[22]

The electric power industry estimated that by the late 1980s more than $15 million a year was being spent to study the health effects of electromagnetic radiation.[23] One of the more sensible scientists in this area, Granger Morgan of Carnegie-Mellon University, thinks this is money well spent.[24] We are less enthusiastic when we look at our electric bill. To us, the evidence remains too inconsistent and potentially misleading for us to unplug our electric blankets or to give up our computer terminals.

Some researchers do not even take the time to go through the motions of questionable statistical methodology to produce positive results. Although comparatively rare, simple fraud is sometimes used to obtain "positive" results. Alexander Kohn has produced a meticulously documented study of examples of such fraud, which involves a growing number of research institutions, such as Emory University, the University of Rochester, Sloan-Kettering Institute,

[20]Robert Pool, "Is There an EMF-Cancer Connection," *Science*, September 7, 1990, pp. 1096–98.

[21]A good overview of various studies is given by A. Ahlbom et al., *Biological Effects of Power Line Fields*, New York State Powerlines Project, Scientific Advisory Final Report, July 1, 1987.

[22]C. Dennis Robinette et al., "Effects upon Health of Occupational Exposure to Microwave Radiation (RADAR)," *American Journal of Epidemiology*, July 1980, pp. 39–53.

[23]Electric Power Research Institute, "Electric and Magnetic Fields: Humans Health Studies," (Palo Alto, California, November 1989).

[24]Department of Engineering and Public Policy, Carnegie-Mellon University, "Electric and Magnetic Fields from 60-Hertz Electric Power: What Do We Know about Possible Health Risks?" (Pittsburgh, 1989).

and Harvard University.[25] Kohn explains some of that fraud in terms of pressure to produce positive results, but he insightfully points out that little of it would have been possible had the fraudulent results not given the "right" answers—answers that colleagues and superiors wanted to believe.

Even under the most ethical and careful of research protocols that use laboratory animals as proxies for human beings, at least three great assumptions must be made: that the laboratory procedure itself (as apart from the substance in question) is not equivalent to a toxic agent, that substances which cause tumors in laboratory animals also cause cancer in humans, and that there is a way to extrapolate (predict) what fraction of those humans who are exposed to the substance at low doses will contract cancer. Each assumption is problematic.

The presumption that the laboratory procedure is not itself carcinogenic is increasingly suspect. Ames and Gold point out that chronic dosing of rodents and other animals with the maximum tolerated dose of a suspected substance is often the same as a chronic wounding of the animal, long known to be associated with cancer in and of itself.[26] The maximum tolerated dose is the dose that causes measurable toxicity but not immediate death; the effect of such a general assault on the body of a laboratory animal is not known in any detail.

The jump from laboratory animals to people remains murky territory for the simple reason that the substance in question may never have been observed to cause cancer in people. The questionable nature of the assumption is illustrated by the fact that some substances that cause tumors in rats do not cause tumors in mice (a very closely related species), much less in people.

Finally, the extrapolation from very high doses to low doses is generally done with linear models which presume that, say, halving

[25]Alexander Kohn, *False Prophets: Fraud and Error in Science and Medicine* (Oxford: Blackwell, 1988). A fascinating account of fraud, which involved painting the skin of laboratory animals, is given in J. Hixson, *The Patchwork Mouse* (Garden City, N.Y.: Anchor/Doubleday, 1976).

[26]Bruce N. Ames and Lois S. Gold, "Too Many Rodent Carcinogens: Mitogenesis Increases Mutagenesis," *Science*, August 31, 1990, pp. 970–71. See also Ronald B. Scott, *Cancer: The Facts* (New York: Oxford University Press, 1979). Repeated trauma, scarring, assaults to the immune system, and infection are all known to be associated with cancer.

the dose will result in a halving of the cancer rate. As we will explore in greater detail in the next chapter, linear extrapolation is usually done not because it is thought to be necessarily correct but because it is thought to be simple or conservative. In other words, a halving of a dose of a toxin may not cut the incidence of cancer by one-half but by a much greater amount. The response curves for saccharin and formaldehyde, for example, are known to be nonlinear, and it is now fairly evident that the same is true for dioxin.

For these and perhaps other reasons, cancer assessment is biased in favor of finding suspected causes of cancer. Nevertheless, the story of human cancer and food additives is fairly simple: after decades of research, the scientific consensus concerning the health hazard of food additives is that it is roughly zero. In 1981 David A. Dunnette, citing evidence from the *Journal of the National Cancer Institute* and other sources, concluded that the cancer risk associated with food additives is roughly nil.[27] At the time of the Alar scare, Sanford Miller, dean of the Graduate School of Biomedical Sciences at the University of Texas at San Antonio, was quoted as follows:

> The risk of pesticide residues to consumers is effectively zero. This is what some fourteen scientific societies representing over 100,000 microbiologists, toxicologists and food scientists said at the time of the ridiculous Alar scare. But we were ignored.[28]

Miller went on to point out that any evidence of injury to consumers has come from the extrapolation of harm done to people, such as farmers, who handle (often improperly) large volumes of pesticides. He also believes that the real tragedy of the scare over food additives is that attention has been directed away from some real problems with food, such as problems of microbiological poisoning from salmonella and botulism.[29]

[27]David A. Dunnette, "Assessing Risks and Preventing Disease From Environmental Chemicals," *Journal of Community Health*, Fall 1989, pp. 169–86.

[28]Warren T. Brookes, "EPA's Misguided Hysteria over Pesticide Risks," *Human Events*, April 21, 1990, p. 9.

[29]Telephone interview conducted by our research assistant, William Jordan, May 6, 1991.

Asbestos

Asbestos is another substance that has generated irrational fears of cancer on the part of the public. Millions of people have assumed that asbestos is a potent carcinogen ever since it was demonstrated in the 1950s to cause lung tumors in asbestos miners. A new industry concerned with inspection and removal of asbestos from buildings has evolved under a mandate from the EPA, which administers the Asbestos Hazard Emergency Response Act of 1986 (AHERA). Conservative estimates are that it will cost at least $53 billion to remedy asbestos problems in approximately three-quarters of a million public and commercial buildings over 30 years. Other estimates run as much as 10 times higher.[30]

A recent article in *Science* offers significant insights into the asbestos question.[31] The institutional affiliations of the article's researchers include the University of Vermont; the Research Institute of Pulmonary and Renal Biopathology and Toxicology in Creteil, France; the School of Hygiene and Public Health at Johns Hopkins University; the Institute of Occupational Medicine in Edinburgh, Scotland; and the Department of Internal Medicine at Yale University School of Medicine. The article points out that asbestos is a broad commercial term for a group of naturally occurring silicates that crystallize into fibers that are in general either serpentine or amphibole. About 90 percent of the serpentine class is composed of chrysotile fibers. The authors indicate that the two classes of fibers differ. The more rarely occurring rod-like amphibole fibers penetrate the lung tissue more readily than the curly chrysotile fibers, which can occur in bundles and are more easily intercepted by parts of the body such as the nose before they are able to penetrate lung tissue. A probable reason for the decreased toxicity from chrysotile fibers is that they are soft and flexible and do not tend to penetrate lung tissue as readily as amphibole fibers, which

---

[30]Some of these estimates are reviewed by M. Corn (director of the Division of Environmental Health Engineering, School of Hygiene and Public Health, Johns Hopkins University) in a paper presented before the 22nd International Congress on Occupational Health, Sydney, Australia, September 1986. Of course, the wide range of estimates points to the speculative nature of cost and benefit calculation for environmental programs.

[31]B. T. Mossman et al., "Asbestos: Scientific Developments and Implications for Public Policy," *Science*, January 9, 1990, pp. 294–300.

are hard and brittle. The two types of asbestos also differ chemically because chrysotile is a magnesium silicate while amphibole contains iron magnesium silicate. Many countries in the European Community stringently regulate the importation of amphibole, but U.S. federal policy does not distinguish between the two types of asbestos.

The *Science* article points out that the concentration of airborne asbestos fibers in schools and public buildings is approximately 1 percent of the permissible exposure (0.2 fibers per cubic centimeter of air) that OSHA allows in the workplace. Before regulation, levels as high as 100 fibers per cubic centimeter were not uncommon in the workplace. Furthermore, with few exceptions the predominant form of asbestos found in buildings is the more benign chrysotile type. Thus despite use of a linear extrapolation from high to low doses to calculate risk factors, the combined data from six published risk estimates—only one of which took into account the difference in pathogenicity between amphibole and chrysotile—indicate that the risk to schoolchildren is minuscule at present levels of airborne asbestos (perhaps one-thousandth the risk of a whooping cough vaccination).

Finally, the article reports that in a survey of 17,800 insulation workers with mixed fiber exposure, 471 were found with lung tumors. Of those, 467 were smokers; 4 workers in 17,800 (or 0.02 percent) were nonsmokers with tumors.

The clear implication is that only insignificant numbers of those workers would have shown any effects at all had they not been smokers. Should public policy be formulated that in essence taxes nonsmokers to reduce health risks to smokers? We think not, when both the government and private sectors have clearly communicated to the public the medical evidence that smoking is akin to slow suicide. Be that as it may, we stress again that, even here, the weak causal data refer to an occupational exposure many times greater than the AHERA-regulated nonoccupational exposure that might be found in schools and public buildings.

Therefore, it is reasonable to conclude there is little danger either to our schoolchildren or to the general public from asbestos now in buildings. In fact, removing asbestos could in itself be a greater hazard than leaving it where it is, since removal will stir up the existing asbestos fibers. Even executives of asbestos removal companies such as Advatex (which has had a recent compound annual growth rate in operating income of more than 20 percent) concede that asbestos need not be disturbed unless demolition or refurbishing is being undertaken.[32] Of greater immediate tragic consequence is the conclusion of Malcolm Ross of the U.S. Geological Survey. Ross speculates that the faulty O-ring in the ill-fated space shuttle Challenger was a direct result of replacing the previously used ring because of an unwarranted fear of asbestos-based putty.[33]

Fortunately, the EPA has reportedly changed course on asbestos removal, and is now leaning more toward coating, encapsulation, or encasement rather than removal.[34] While the necessity of even those measures is far from clear, science may have finally had an impact on EPA policy. On the other hand, the EPA's change of heart may have been produced simply by the impending financial ruin of many school systems (especially of parochial schools). Whatever the cause, it is surely welcome.

Also welcome is this development: in October 1991 the U.S. District Court of Appeals in New Orleans struck down major parts of the EPA ban on asbestos products and ruled that the agency had not properly weighed the costs and benefits of asbestos prohibition. Further, the court ruled that some of the planned substitutes may pose a toxic risk as great as or greater than asbestos itself.[35]

J. Corbett McDonald and Alison McDonald of the National Heart and Lung Institute in London, England, summed up the fiscal waste in asbestos policy very well:

> To those of us who have spent our lives in public health research, it seems strange and sad that a country with one of the highest infant mortality rates in the Western world and no shortage of other health and behavioral problems should commit billions of dollars to the questionable control

[32]Marc Reisch, "Asbestos Removal Firm Expects Future Growth," *Chemical and Engineering News*, March 12, 1990, p. 18.

[33]See the comprehensive study by Michael Bennett, *The Asbestos Racket: An Environmental Parable* (Bellevue, Wash.: Free Enterprise Press, 1991). For more detail on the media contribution to the asbestos scare, see "The Real Asbestos Horror Story," *AIM Report*, September-A, 1990 (Accuracy in Media, Washington, D.C.).

[34]See Dan McInnis, "EPA Changes Course on Asbestos Removal," *Human Events*, October 20, 1990, p. 11.

[35]"Court Overturns EPA's Asbestos Ban," *Science*, November 15, 1991, p. 318.

of a minuscule or nonexistent health risk. Perhaps the real problems are too difficult.[36]

Dioxin

One of the most notorious incidents in the history of the U.S. environmental movement is the case of Love Canal. The canal, built in the late 19th century by entrepreneur William Love to circumvent Niagara Falls and provide cheap power, was a trench about 40 feet deep, 20 yards wide, and a mile long. Love's resources were not capable of completing the project and the canal became a waste dump for Hooker Chemical in the 1930s and 1940s.

In 1952, while under threat of eminent-domain proceedings by the city of Niagara Falls, Hooker deeded the land to the city for use by the school board. The company insisted that all transfer papers contain a warning of the chemicals buried under the property. Nevertheless, school facilities were constructed, sewers were laid, and the integrity of the fill was breached. It is little wonder that wastes and odors began to escape.[37]

Hooker Chemical was, of course, convicted in the media by writers such as Michael Brown, who noted in *Atlantic Monthly* that part of the residue in the dump came from the manufacture of 2,4,5 trichlorophenol, whose production might make dioxin as an unwanted by-product.[38] Brown described dioxin as a chemical whose potency was "beyond imagination" and stated that if three ounces of it were distributed among a million people, all would die. This rather dire prediction was shown to be false when an explosion at Seveso, Italy, in July 1976 distributed three pounds of dioxin over 700 acres of that town located north of Milan. Since then over 30,000 blood tests have been done on the residents, and one of the tests detected the highest level of dioxin ever found in a human being. Nevertheless, in the face of continued medical surveillance, the only pathologic effect found was chloracne, an acne associated with exposure to chlorinated chemicals.

[36]J. Corbett McDonald and Alison D. McDonald, "Asbestos and Carcinogenicity," *Science*, August 24, 1990, p. 844.

[37]For an excellent short history of Love Canal, see Richard L. Stroup and Jane S. Shaw, "The Free Market and the Environment," *Public Interest*, Fall 1989, pp. 30–43.

[38]Michael H. Brown, "Love Canal and the Poisoning of America," *Atlantic Monthly*, December 1979, pp. 33–47.

Of course, there were many other investigations at Love Canal. Beverly Paigen, a biologist from the Roswell Institute, claimed that children in the Love Canal area had twice the birth defects, seizures, and skin rashes as did those in a control group. In 1980 a private contractor employed by the state of New York to do a chromosome study claimed that an unusually high percentage of residents had extra pieces of genetic material. Those findings, which caused panic in the area, were generally given greater media attention than the findings of eminent scientists such as Lewis Thomas, chancellor of Sloan-Kettering Institute, who noted that Paigen's report was largely based on anecdotal evidence obtained from a narrowly selected group and consequently, it failed to meet sound scientific standards.[39] Further, a U.S. Department of Health and Human Services follow-up chromosome study of residents failed to find any extra genetic material. A twist to the chromosome affair was reported in the May 28, 1983, issue of *Science,* which noted that a control group composed of other Niagara Falls residents showed a higher incidence of chromosomal damage than did the Love Canal residents.

It has been more than a decade since the media broke the Love Canal story, and we know of not a single accepted scientific study that has shown widespread harm to residents of Love Canal. In a review of the evidence, David Dunnette summarizes the findings as follows:

> In short it appears that the magnitude of public health risk at hazardous waste sites has not yet been demonstrated to be very great and that the public's perception of such risks is not supported by the data.[40]

Interestingly enough, many people are attempting to buy Love Canal homes that were evacuated about a decade ago. In August 1990, 204 applicants vied for ten houses scheduled for sale. However, the Sierra Club and the Natural Resources Defense Council fought the sale in court. They lost in the state court and will probably appeal. A planned suit against the EPA has not yet been filed.[41]

[39]See Michael H. Brown, "A Toxic Ghost Town," *Atlantic,* July 1989, pp. 23–28.
[40]Dunnette, p. 177.
[41]Telephone interview with Jim Simon of NRDC, May 5, 1991.

59

Dioxin continues to remain high on the list of chemophobic concoctions. It is a contaminant of Agent Orange, which was used as a defoliant during the Vietnam War, and has been reputed to cause various kinds of maladies among veterans and others exposed to it. Nevertheless, repeated studies have failed to show a greater incidence of ailments among soldiers who were exposed to the chemical and who have blood concentrations up to seven times higher than soldiers not exposed to the chemical. In short, a number of recent studies appears to show that the risks from dioxin have been ranked too high, and by 1988 the EPA had revised downward about 16-fold its estimate of public health risk from dioxin exposure.[42] Indeed, a series of studies released in 1991 reported no relationship between Agent Orange–related dioxin and "cancer of any kind, liver disease, heart disease, kidney disease, immune system disorders, psychological abnormalities, or nervous system disease."[43] This new scientific consensus concerning dioxin has been echoed by the prestigious journal *Nature*,[44] and the EPA is now reviewing its estimates on the toxicity of dioxin.

In 1990 the EPA and the Food and Drug Administration sponsored a meeting at Cold Spring Harbor, New York, where a group of nearly 40 international experts on dioxin debated issues such as toxicity and exposure. Again, the consensus arrived at was that contemporary risk assessment models did not accurately represent what scientists knew about the chemical's toxicity. As seems to be the trouble in much of the risk assessment literature, the current model for dioxin is linear and the actual dose-response relationship for dioxin is apparently nonlinear. There may be evidence of a cancer relationship at very high exposures but not at low exposures. The new thinking is that dioxin is perhaps only a hundredth as toxic as predicted by the old model.[45] Yet, in the words of a recent report in *Science*, because the chemical is "politically charged," it remains difficult for the EPA to revise downward the assessed risk

[42]See Dunnette, p. 176, and his extensive bibliography.

[43]David J. Hanson, "New Reports Find Little Effect by Agent Orange on Veterans," *Chemical and Engineering News*, April 15, 1991, p. 15.

[44]David Lindley, "Risky Arguments over Cause and Effect," *Nature*, August 9, 1990, p. 507.

[45]David Hanson, "EPA to Take Another Hard Look at Dioxin Health Risk," *Chemical and Engineering News*, April 29, 1991, p. 31.

of dioxin to a level that growing numbers of scientists believe to be reasonable.[46]

But there is hope. In February 1983, the EPA announced it would pay $33 million to buy all homes and businesses in the small Missouri town of Times Beach.[47] The town of roughly 2,000 people had been the site of panic because waste oil containing a small amount of dioxin had been spread on the streets to control dust. But on May 25, 1991, the *Washington Post* reported that Vernon N. Houk, the official who had recommended the evacuation, said that he would not have done so had he known then what he now knows about dioxin. (The *Post* went on to say that Karen Webb, director of the Division of Environmental and Occupational Health at St. Louis University School of Medicine, reported that studies at Times Beach had found no significant chronic illness.)

And in 1991, a long-standing dioxin suit was resolved in favor of the defendant, Monsanto Company. The case had arisen when a train derailment spilled about 19,000 gallons of a wood preservative that contained minute traces of dioxin (the highest level found was about 45 parts per billion). The original jury award to 65 plaintiffs had been $16.25 million, but it was overturned by the Fifth District Appellate Court. Law professor David G. Owen of the University of South Carolina said that the significance of the verdict might lie in the court's refusal to allow damages based on fear alone.[48]

The Continuing Phobia

Dioxin represents the problem of the "measurement mania" of chemophobia. In a March 26, 1990, interview in *Fortune* magazine, the CEO of Georgia Pacific Company commented that the dioxin produced in the pulp and paper business was in quantities so small that it can be detected only by the most advanced analytical techniques.[49] But as these techniques advance further the mandate to reduce dioxin emissions to nondetectable levels will become

---

[46]Leslie Roberts, "Dioxin Risks Revisited," *Science*, February 8, 1991, pp. 624–26.

[47]Richard L. Stroup, "Environmental Policy," *Regulation*, 1988, no. 3, p. 43.

[48]David Hanson, "Monsanto Wins Reversal of TCDD Damages," *Chemical and Engineering News*, June 24, 1991, p. 6.

[49]"What Is a Non-Detectable Level of Dioxin?" *Fortune*, March 26, 1990, p. 88.

virtually impossible to satisfy—detection techniques may eventually reach the molecular level.

A phobia is defined as an irrational fear. While there are deaths from chemical explosions, refinery fires, and other rare events, the toll in human life is minuscule compared to the lives saved and the comfort provided by products of the chemical and chemical-related industries. The economic loss that chemophobia exacts from the American people is regrettable, but the loss of freedom that results when government is asked to eliminate all risks will no doubt prove even more destructive in the long run. To paraphrase Aaron Wildavsky, when we ask another party to bear our risks, we automatically transfer some of our freedom to that party. And when that party is the government, the transfer is likely to be permanent.[50]

[50]Aaron Wildavsky, "No Risk Is the Highest Risk of All," *American Scientist*, January–February 1979, pp. 32–37.

5. A Multibillion-Dollar Radon Scare

Most Americans know little about radon. Despite that fact, or perhaps because of it, America is falling into a radon panic. Spurred by the media, Americans have grown increasingly fearful that mysterious but deadly gases lurk in their basements. Radon detectors of doubtful worth are peddled at corner drug stores, and books such as Linda Mason Hunter's *The Healthy Home* teach us how to avoid radon's terrors.[1]

The radon scare has benefited regulators as well as entrepreneurs. It has allowed the Environmental Protection Agency (EPA) to begin regulating one of our last bastions of privacy, the home. And many other government agencies have gotten into the act: the Departments of Energy, Housing and Urban Development, and Veterans' Affairs; the Federal Housing Authority; and even the National Park Service. Unbeknown to the public, however, the scientific evidence for the radon alarm is far from compelling.

Fact and Fancy

Radon is a naturally occurring radioactive gas derived from uranium deposits in the ground.[2] Its surface concentration varies from place to place because of differences in soil structure, the presence of cracks or fissures in the earth, and other geological factors. Radon tends to accumulate in mines and caves, putting miners at greater risk from lung cancer than above-ground workers. Nevertheless, radon can be detected in at least minute quantities virtually everywhere.

The half-life (the time needed for a radioactive substance to decay to one-half its original activity) of the longest-lived radon isotope is less than four days, and the adverse health effects come not from

---

[1]Linda Mason Hunter, *The Healthy Home* (Emmaus, Pa.: Rodale Press, 1989).

[2]Some other naturally occurring sources of radiation include cosmic rays, tritium, beryllium, and potassium. See U.N. Scientific Committee on the Effects of Atomic Radiation, *Sources and Effects of Ionizing Radiation* (New York: United Nations, 1977).

radon itself but from certain isotopes created during radon decay. Those isotopes are referred to as "radon daughters"; the most prevalent of them is polonium, which is chemically reactive and has the ability to stick to the lining of bronchial passages. Like many other naturally occurring products (such as salt), those isotopes can be fatal in sufficiently large doses. The question is not whether radon daughters can cause adverse health effects, but rather how large a dose of them distributed over what period of time is needed to do so. Because radon can become concentrated in closed above-ground spaces such as homes, the public-policy question is whether radon exposure during ordinary living in the typical home endangers public health. Actually, a more pertinent question is whether low concentrations of radon might instead be beneficial.

The radon scare in the United States began in the 1970s when the Public Health Service discovered that high levels of radon were accumulating in homes built over uranium mill tailings and in land reclaimed from phosphate mines in Florida.[3] The concern became full-blown in 1984 when a nuclear power engineer named Stanley Watras set off nuclear monitors at his job because of his exposure to high radon concentration in his Pennsylvania home. Media attention given to this incident led to an immediate concern that the radon concentrations in other homes could be high enough to pose a public health hazard. By the mid-1980s the radon scare had passed into full media sensationalism with the appearance of feature stories such as "The House that Glowed" (*Health*), "Why Did My Sister Get Lung Cancer?" (*Saturday Evening Post*), and "The Colorless Odorless Killer" (*Time*).

It is difficult, however, to assess the hazard of exposure to radon. Because controlled experimentation on human beings is not ethical, statistical data must be interpreted and used to predict the probable consequences of exposure at low levels. If high levels of radon can lead to lung cancer in miners, do levels that are considerably lower than those found in mines cause any appreciable harm? Interpretation of modern data on miners, furthermore, suggests there may be some synergistic interaction between smoking and radon exposure.

---

[3]David J. Hanson, "Radon Tagged as Cancer Hazard by Most Studies, Researchers," *Chemical and Engineering News*, February 6, 1989, pp. 7–13.

Should public policy attempt to protect smokers, since their smoking is voluntary and done despite health warnings?

Given those uncertainties, one might, like some radon alarmists, adopt the stance that virtually no radon can be allowed as a matter of public health policy. Studies on the effects of background radiation on human populations, however, tend to undermine the zero-tolerance stand. In 1980 the High Background Radiation Research Group reported in *Science* the results of a massive study of Chinese living in two different regions, one with high natural background radiation and one with low.[4] In all, more than 140,000 people were studied—about 70,000 per region. The whole-body exposure to natural radiation experienced by the inhabitants of the high-radiation region was more than two times that experienced by the inhabitants of the other region.

The China study is important because it allows contrasts to be drawn between two populations that are similar in most respects, except for greatly different levels of exposure to natural background radiation. Thus the study approximates the conditions of a controlled experiment. Furthermore, since several thousand people in each region reported that their ancestors had resided in the same area for over 16 generations, the study is capable of assessing any long-term genetic difference between the two populations.

The findings of the China study do not support the view that differences in natural above-ground background radiation have any appreciable short- or long-term health consequences over the range of exposure studied. In the research group's words, the study "did not demonstrate any significant difference between inhabitants living in the high-background and control [low-background] areas."[5] The authors added that perhaps a larger sample size was needed to show any adverse health effects, but we suspect that this caveat is merely a way of asking for more research funding. It is difficult to imagine, from a statistical point of view, any change in results from a study even more massive than the one conducted.

The China radiation study illustrates a vital point in the radon controversy: the effect of radiation exposure is probably nonlinear.

[4]High Background Radiation Research Group, "Health Survey in High Background Radiation Areas in China," *Science*, August 22, 1980, pp. 877–80.

[5]Ibid, p. 880.

In other words, an incremental halving of exposure, say, does not necessarily lead to an incremental halving of the number of occurrences of diseases such as lung cancer. The China data clearly indicate that a halving of radiation exposure—at least within the range studied—could yield no significant health differences at all. In fact, some recent animal investigations also tend to show that the health effects of low levels of exposure are much less than would be predicted linearly from higher levels of exposure.[6] In short, it is questionable whether the health effects of high-radon exposure levels can be extended linearly to low levels.

Statisticians view simple linear extrapolation as a naive way to predict most phenomena. It would not be very effective, for example, to draw a straight line through the Dow-Jones Industrial Averages of today and yesterday and to extend that line to predict tomorrow's Dow. Experience would soon prove that such a technique almost never works. In most cases, therefore, linear extrapolation is used only by the naive or when the level of information is so low that no other technique seems possible.

But linear extrapolation is exactly the technique that the EPA uses to predict the health effects of low levels of radon exposure. A paper by J. S. Puskin and Y. Yang, both of the EPA, illustrates the technique: the EPA relative-risk model "assumes that the incremental risk of a given effect (e.g., lung-cancer mortality) associated with a given exposure is linearly proportional to the baseline rate of the effect in the population."[7] The EPA projects the consequences of low-level radon exposure by linearly extrapolating from the consequences of high-level exposure.

On the basis of this method, the EPA has concluded that it is dangerous to live in a home with 4 picocuries (pCi) of radiation per liter of air as measured in the basement or at the foundation. The fact that this level is determined by linear extrapolation is not its only flaw. Because the radon measurement is short term and taken in the basement or at the foundation of a house, it may have no relation to levels actually experienced in living areas or by people who do not spend much time at home. The EPA claims that its

[6]Hanson.

[7]J. S. Puskin and Y. Yang, "A Retrospective Look at Rn-Induced Lung Cancer Mortality from the Viewpoint of a Relative Risk Model," *Health Physics*, June 1988, 635–43.

methods of extrapolation and measurement are merely conservative, but one suspects that it says so to avoid embarrassment. The
EPA set the 4-pCi-per-liter standard years ago for homes located
on uranium tailings; since a great deal of money was spent to clean
up those homes, there would be many red-faced bureaucrats if the
EPA changed its recommendation at this late date.[8]

How much radiation is 4 pCi per liter? Unfortunately, there is
no direct conversion between millirems (used in the China study)
and picocuries, so the EPA standard cannot be compared directly
to the China data. This lack of direct comparability is because "picocuries" refers to the number of nuclear disintegrations per second
while "millirems" measures the biological consequences of radiation. If one imagines a rainstorm, the analogy is roughly that "picocuries" refers to the number of drops of rain per second, while
millirems refers to how wet a person gets. The complicated multi-
step decay of radon prevents any direct comparison of the two
measures.

Still, 4 pCi per liter is not very much radiation. In the United
States an ordinary glass of drinking water contains about 0.3 pCi
of radioactive material, while a glass of milk contains about 18
pCi. The radiation levels in the China study were much higher.
According to the research group's estimates, the ground concentration of the radium-226 isotope in the high-background area was
between 1,700 and 2,000 pCi per kilogram of soil, while the concentration for the low-background area was between 300 and 900 pCi
per kilogram. Indeed, there seems to be no unusual incidence of
lung-cancer deaths for U.S. uranium miners when exposures are
below 12,000 pCi per liter of air.[9] One does not have to know what
a picocurie is to know that 12,000 is a lot bigger than 4.

Douglas Brookins, a geologist at the University of New Mexico,
attempts to defend the EPA standard in his recent book, *The Indoor
Radon Problem.*[10] The book is an excellent example of a radon scare
piece—it is superficially plausible so long as the fine print is
ignored. Brookins claims, for example, that between 1 and 5 percent

[8]Tim Beardsley, "Radon Retried," *Scientific American*, December 1988, p. 18.

[9]David Hanson, "EPA Urges Testing of Homes for Radon," *Chemical and Engineering News*, September 19, 1988, p. 5.

[10]Douglas Brookins, *The Indoor Radon Problem* (New York: Columbia University
Press, 1990).

of people living in houses with 4 pCi of radon per liter of air will die of lung cancer. This prediction, of course, is based on the usual linear extrapolation; it also presumes that people spend their lives at the point of radon measurement—the basement. The fine print, moreover, indicates that the people in question are assumed to live in the same house for 70 years and to spend 70 to 80 percent of their time in it. Confronted with such a grim existence, a person might be tempted to take up smoking, perhaps multiplying the radon risk. That is especially true if the person is unfortunate enough to live in North Dakota, a state with one of the nation's highest background-radiation levels. But North Dakotans have the highest average longevity in America, so they might actually have to live out the whole of their somber 70 years under the threat of radon.

It should come as little surprise that the EPA's 4-pCi-per-liter action level is likely to be very costly. A recent EPA study of seven states indicates that nearly one-third of the homes exceed that level. EPA recommends that the owners of those houses install vents and other remedial devices to lower the radon levels. If those figures stand up to further sampling, and if modifications to homes cost between $500 and $5,000 each, the total bill for fixing America's radon "problem" could be in the range of $10 billion—$100 billion. Even if the total cost is half that amount, the expenditure is still so staggering that the EPA is said to fear a homeowners' movement that would seek a monumental government bailout—creating a new Superfund or S&L crisis. Even without a bailout, the government would have to pay a substantial sum to eliminate radon from public buildings. Half the schools recently sampled by the EPA, for instance, were found to have problem levels of radon in at least one classroom. Cleanup costs could easily run as high as $10,000 per school, especially in view of the EPA's stated desire to lower radon levels in the classrooms to below 1 pCi per liter of air.[11] Perhaps worse, if we follow EPA's suggestions that homes be certified as radon safe before their sale, an unknown fraction of the American people's capital stock might be destroyed; it is likely that many homes could not meet the EPA action level even after modification.

[11]Linda Chavez, "Sick Schools," *New York Times*, November 5, 1989.

Scientific Opposition

Fortunately, an impressive array of scientists is taking a stand against the EPA on the radon question. Anthony Nero of Lawrence Berkeley Laboratory, for example, estimates that only 2 percent of U.S. homes exceed 8 pCi per liter, a level that he finds would place the radon hazard on a par with falls or fires in the home.[12] Other scientists—such as John Harley, retired director of the Department of Energy's Environmental Measurement Laboratory—agree that the EPA action level should be raised by a factor of two to five.[13]

Still other scientists believe that low levels of radon exposure may actually be beneficial to health. Bernard Cohen of the University of Pittsburgh examined data on lung cancer and radon exposure in over 400 counties in the United States; he concluded that lung-cancer deaths were significantly *lower* in high-exposure areas than in low-exposure areas. Critics contend that Cohen's data are faulty, but low doses of some toxic substances actually do stimulate the immune system. That effect is called "hormesis," and it has been known since the 19th century.[14] In 1979 a conference in Oakland, California, discussed over one thousand references to the hormetic effects of low doses of radiation. But even if low levels of radiation are not beneficial, they seem at least to be less harmful than is often supposed. According to Leonard Sagan, a proponent of the possibility of low-radiation hormesis, "Accumulated experience has tended to reduce fears of the mutagenic effects of low-dose ionizing radiation."[15] Sagan notes that human beings are about one-fourth as sensitive to radiation as was previously expected from forecasts using studies on rats, that statistical studies of survivors of atomic bombing have failed to produce statistically significant results, and that the ability of human DNA to repair itself is indeed remarkable. In other words, even if the claims of radiation hormesis are not

[12]Anthony V. Nero, Jr., "Estimated Risk of Lung Cancer from Exposure to Radon Decay Products in U.S. Homes: A Brief Review," *Atmospheric Environment*, October 1988, pp. 2205–11.

[13]Richard A. Kerr, "Radon Survey Seen as Misleading by Some Scientists," *Science*, September 23, 1988, pp. 1594–95.

[14]For a debate on the hormesis issue, see Leonard A. Sagan, "On Radiation, Paradigms, and Hormesis," and Sheldon Wolff, "Are Radiation Effects Hormetic?" in *Science*, August 11, 1989, pp. 574ff.

[15]Sagan, p. 574.

borne out by future studies, the zero-tolerance model of radiation exposure is becoming increasingly suspect.[16]

The late Warren T. Brookes reported the following conversation with Bernard Cohen:

> However, as Dr. Cohen told me, "You understand, radon is the most serious risk with which the EPA is now dealing." "But, Dr. Cohen," I said, "you just got through telling me that residential radon poses no public health risk!" "That's right," he said.[17]

By the fall of 1990 the criticism against the EPA had reached the editorial pages of *Science*, which censured the agency for its plans for a nationwide campaign against radon. The predicted cost of radon "correction" given in the editorial was $10,000 per home.[18] The editorial went on to mention the uncertain effects of radon on miners given the confounding effects of smoking, to cite Bernard Cohen's data that fail to show adverse health effects of radon, and to deplore the needless expenditure and anxiety that the radon program has generated. Undeterred, in July 1991 the EPA went so far as to set the maximum radon 222 level in drinking water at 300 pCi per liter. Since radon from drinking water contributes less than 5 percent of total indoor radon exposures, the regulation is expected to have virtually no effect on indoor radon exposure. The cost of this regulation, however, has been estimated at more than $12 billion in capital costs alone.[19]

Mankind has lived with natural radiation for millions of years. We should be allowed to continue to do so, peacefully, without fear, and without a radiation inspector at the door or a radiation detector in the basement.

---

[16]See also Melvin A. Benarde, *Our Precarious Habitat: Fifteen Years Later* (New York: John Wiley and Sons, 1989), p. 388.

[17]Warren T. Brookes, "Bush Clean Air Program Is Full of Risks for Economy," *Human Events*, September 16, 1989, p. 11.

[18]P. H. Abelson, "Uncertainties about Health Effects of Radon," *Science*, October 10, 1990, p. 353.

[19]M. W. Tikkanen, "Safe Drinking Water Act Update: Radon Technologies, Risk Reduction, Costs." (Paper presented before the 34th Rocky Mountain Conference on Analytical Chemistry, Denver, Colo., August 4, 1992.)

6. The Greenhouse Effect: What Is the Real Issue?

The idea of an enhanced greenhouse effect (or global warming) is an old one. The foundations for the theory go back at least to 1896 and the Swedish scientist Svante Arrhenius, who calculated, on a theoretical basis, that an increase in carbon dioxide might result in an increase in global temperature. The idea did not become a cause célèbre with the public until the 1980s, when several unusually warm years prompted warnings from some scientists that economic activities might be affecting the climate.

Fossil and tree-ring data both indicate that variations in climate have persisted for millions of years and have exhibited considerable random fluctuations within long cycles of 100,000 years. A cycle consists of a period of glaciation lasting about 90,000 years followed by a period of warming lasting about 10,000 years. The present relatively warm interglacial period appears to have begun about 11,000 years ago. Many scientists wonder if another period of extreme cooling is not overdue.

Within those long swings in temperature there is considerable variability, which has much of the character of randomness. Over the past two thousand years, there have been several epochs when the mean temperature of the air was significantly cooler or warmer than it is today. For example, from the middle of the 15th to the early 19th centuries, cooler-than-normal air temperature led to a period that has come to be called the Little Ice Age. And in two periods that occurred about 6,000 and 1,000 years ago, the air temperature was on average 1°–3° Fahreheit warmer than it is today.

How Well Do We Understand the Weather?

Our scientific understanding of why those and other fluctuations in temperature occurred in the past is quite meager, and there is no agreed-on theory that explains them all. Changes in the earth's orbit, volcanic eruption, sunspot activity, geologic movements, and many other factors are mentioned in the meteorological literature. In fact, understanding of the weather is so unsatisfactory that 90-day forecasting even with the help of large super-computers is only slightly better than tossing dice. Over the past two decades, the National Weather Service has a record of being correct about 38 times in 99 when forecasting whether the temperature will be above normal, near normal, or below normal for the next 90 days. The use of some random device would have produced the correct forecast 33 times in 99.[1]

The devilish complexity of weather is illustrated by the "butterfly effect," a name Edward Lorenz gave to weather disturbances. Lorenz, a distinguished research meteorologist who spent many years attempting to create mathematical models that could be used by computers to understand weather, discovered in the early 1960s that the nonlinear equations used to model weather could deteriorate into tracking patterns that would later be called "chaotic dynamics." Unlike the deterministic and predictable equations of motion of Newtonian physics, these weather models could exhibit patterns that were very difficult to distinguish from randomness and that were extremely sensitive to the starting values given to them. The models were so sensitive that Lorenz likened them to a butterfly beating its wings in some remote place and affecting weather many miles away.[2] The weather, Lorenz discovered, was much more complicated than had been imagined.

Even the relatively simple task of taking consistent measurements of temperature is difficult. One problem is that many official weather stations are located close to urban areas. It is warmer in these areas because cities tend to act as heat traps. As cities expand toward weather stations, the warming effect of urban areas on official temperature measures increases. It is not entirely clear how large an adjustment needs to be made to account for this urban heat-island effect.[3]

[1]Richard A. Kerr, "A New Way to Forecast Next Season's Climate," *Science*, April 7, 1989, pp. 30–31.

[2]An excellent description of Lorenz's work is given in James Gleick, *Chaos: Making a New Science* (New York: Viking, 1988).

[3]See Richard A. Kerr, "The Global Warming Is Real," *Science*, February 3, 1989, p. 603.

Is the Greenhouse at Hand?

Yet in the face of these difficulties in understanding either the past or future of weather, it is said that a "greenhouse effect" is about to threaten the earth. The enhanced greenhouse effect predicts that the increasing amounts of water vapor, carbon dioxide, methane, ozone, nitrogen oxides, and freons produced by man will cause solar radiation reaching the earth to become trapped in the form of heat, thus raising the mean temperature of the globe. The effect is purported to work in much the same way as does solar radiation trapped by glass in a greenhouse or an automobile. Environmentalists say this warming of the earth will lead to dire ecological consequences, such as an increase in sea levels because of melting polar ice, the destruction of large forest and farming regions, the loss of water for irrigation because of increased evaporation, and changes in precipitation patterns resulting in droughts. Indeed, speculation on the effects of global warming has led to international conferences and cries for government programs to reduce the use of fossil fuels and to take advantage of the ability of trees to take up carbon dioxide by increasing the size of forests.

An often-repeated scare story relating to global warming is that the sea level will rise rapidly because of glacial melting. Some predicted consequences of that melting are the flooding of low-lying places such as Bangladesh, parts of Florida, and many coastal cities. At the February 1991 annual meeting of the American Association for the Advancement of Science, Nils-Axel Morner of Stockholm University addressed this prediction with skepticism.[4] He noted that there was simply not enough water in mid-latitude glaciers to cause such a rise in the sea level, and that a 4° Fahrenheit increase in average temperature might cause a rise in average sea level of as much as 4 inches. That would not have terrible consequences.

The media give relatively little play to the fact that many reputable scientists do not agree that an atmospheric crisis is at hand. Indeed, the situation is reminiscent of the furor that was generated over the concept of nuclear winter as promoted by Carl Sagan and others.

---

[4]John P. Wiley, "Phenomena, Comments, and Notes," *Smithsonian*, April 1991, p. 26.

The idea was later roundly debunked, but unlike the initial claim, the debunking was mostly ignored.[5]

The case for any enhanced greenhouse effect rests on the ability to predict what effect the greenhouse gases will have on long-term weather patterns (perhaps decades away), a forecasting ability that plainly does not exist. The controversy is not whether the gases are able to trap heat, but whether those gases will trap a significant amount of heat given the profusion of other things that are going on in the atmosphere at the same time. Greenhouse computer models suffer from a bad case of holding too many things constant. Among those things that are ignored, held constant, or perhaps even entered backwards in the models are the effects of clouds, of deep ocean convection currents, and large exogenous and unpredictable events that might more than offset greenhouse warming.

The effect of cloud cover is one of the clearest problems in the models. Anyone who has lived for any period understands that clouds can have an effect on the temperature. In the summer, a cloudy day tends to be cooler than a clear day because the cloud cover blocks the warming effects of the sun. In the winter, nights with cloud cover are generally warmer because the clouds tend to trap heat rather than allow it to escape as it does on clear nights. Since both the water vapor released by man and the warming tend to enhance the production of clouds, a pertinent question is whether those clouds will mitigate the warming or make it worse.

It turns out that most greenhouse models assume that clouds will make the warming worse. But recent satellite data show that clouds, on balance, tend to cool rather than heat the earth.[6] In short, there may be a self-regulating feedback mechanism that many greenhouse models have backwards. After examining 14 greenhouse models, Robert Cess et al. concluded that the climate effects of greenhouse gases varied by a factor of three primarily because of their differences in cloud modeling,[7] a fact that, among others, caused a leading modeler, Michael Schlesinger of Oregon

[5]Russell Seitz, " 'Nuclear Winter' Melts Down," *National Interest*, Fall 1986, pp. 3–17.

[6]V. Ramanathan et al., "Cloud-Radiative Forcing and Climate: Results from the Earth Radiation Budget Experiment," *Science*, January 6, 1989, pp. 57–63.

[7]R. D. Cess et al., "Interpretation of Cloud-Climate Feedback as Produced by 14 Atmospheric General Circulation Models," *Science*, August 4, 1989, pp. 51–16.

State University, to comment: "You have every right to be very, very skeptical of the results [of today's models]. . . . But this is the best that we're doing."[8]

A second problem with the models is their ignorance of the effects of deep ocean currents. About 11,000 years ago, as the last ice age began to abate and the world returned to warmer temperatures, regions of the North Atlantic were struck by dramatic cooling. That cooling was felt most severely in Western Europe, and the period has come to be known as the Younger Dryas (after an Arctic flower). The cause of the cooling, which reached near Ice Age intensity, is postulated to be the melting and breakup of North American and European ice sheets, which dumped great amounts of fresh water into the North Atlantic. Anyone who has used salt on a driveway in the winter knows that fresh water freezes more readily than salt water, and the dumping of fresh water into the North Atlantic is postulated to have created an ice barrier to the Gulf Stream, which ordinarily warms northwestern Europe.[9] But other plausible explanations (some quite recent) have been offered for the Younger Dryas, and the lack of scientific consensus on the issue serves mainly to illustrate our ignorance of the role of the oceans in weather and to help explain why current greenhouse models either ignore ocean circulation and its effect on heat transport or take it into account in very incomplete ways.[10]

A major reason for our ignorance of the role of oceans in affecting weather arises from the fact that while atmospheric readings of air circulation and temperature have been taken in most land areas of the world on a daily basis for many decades, temperature and circulation measures for the oceans have been made only sporadically and certainly not on a worldwide basis. Without such data, any prediction regarding the effect of oceans on weather is bound to be fraught with uncertainty.

The effects of the oceans on weather remain uncharted territory. As Bette Hileman of *Chemical and Engineering News* points out:

[8]Quoted in Richard A. Kerr, "How to Fix the Clouds in Greenhouse Models," *Science*, January 6, 1989, pp. 28–29.

[9]Stephen H. Schneider, "Climate Modeling," *Scientific American*, May 1987, pp. 72–80.

[10]N. J. Shackleton, "Deep Trouble for Climate Change, *Nature*, December 7, 1989, pp. 616–17.

> Trying to understand global warming without factoring in
> deep ocean circulation and changes in ocean heat transport
> may be analogous to trying to understand how a bird flies
> without studying its wing structure.[11]

Finally, periods of glaciation (ice ages) have been correlated with the amount of solar radiation received by the earth. A report written by William A. Nierenberg, director emeritus of Scripps Institute of Oceanography; Robert Jastrow, founder and former director of the Goddard Institute for Space Studies; and Frederick Seitz, past president of the National Academy of Sciences, attributes the very modest and questionable warming of 0.5° Celsius over the past century to increased solar activity. The report, which has been given additional support by Jerome Namias of Scripps and Reginald Newell of the Massachusetts Institute of Technology, has been dismissed as "noisy junk science" by Jerry Mahlman, director of the National Oceanic and Atmospheric Administration's Geophysical Fluid Dynamics Laboratory, where one of the major greenhouse models was developed. Incidentally, the Nierenberg report included a prediction that solar activity would decrease in the next century and would lead to a small ice age, and that any greenhouse effect would help to mitigate this predicted cooling.[12]

The unusually warm and dry summer of 1988 and its concurrent media coverage have clearly been the proximate causes of the public attention given to the greenhouse effect. Did the weather of this uncommon year signal the onset of the greenhouse? While almost all meteorological scientists say no, the greatest media attention was given to James Hansen who, as director of NASA's Goddard Institute for Space Studies, commanded great visibility. In the late summer of 1988, Hansen created headlines in most major newspapers and appeared on network news with the message that global warming was here. Apparently, most of the more prudent climatologists who were doing research on this issue were appalled by

---

[11]Bette Hileman, "Global Warming," *Chemical and Engineering News*, March 13, 1989, pp. 25–44.

[12]For a discussion of this report ("Scientific Perspectives on the Greenhouse Problem," George C. Marshall Institute, Washington, D.C.), see Leslie Roberts, "Global Warming: Blaming the Sun," *Science*, November 24, 1989, pp. 992–93.

Hansen's statements.[13] It seems fair to summarize their position with the remark of scientist Michael Schlesinger, who characterized our ability to detect global warming as "near zero."[14]

Yet there is an increase in the number of "concerned" scientists and media figures who call for changes in social policy, such as reducing the use of fossil fuels, constructing more expensive buildings to improve heating efficiency, increasing research on nonfossil fuels, imposing emissions fees on fossil fuels, and increasing auto efficiency.[15] Stephen Schneider of the National Center for Atmospheric Research epitomizes the views of scientists who favor immediate social action to counter the perceived greenhouse threat despite the admitted uncertainties of its magnitude. Schneider predicts dire consequences if society should wait another decade before acting to mitigate the greenhouse effect. He also thinks that whether the uncertainties of the magnitude of the greenhouse effect are large enough to delay a policy response is not a scientific judgment but a value judgment.[16]

Of course, many people other than scientists advocate action to deal with the threat. Robert Redford, Tom Brokaw, Gary Trudeau, and other worthies took part in a joint meeting with Soviet scientists in August 1988 at Sundance, Utah, to warn of imminent global warming. Politicians such as Norway's Prime Minister Gro Harlem Brundtland and then-Senator Albert Gore issued similar warnings after apparently sniffing an issue with a good deal of potential political mileage. John Hoffman, director of the Environmental Protection Agency's Office of Global Change, opined that "the world can't afford to wait until every last detail is uncovered."[17] The list of people who wish to be included on the greenhouse bandwagon is seemingly endless.

[13]Richard Kerr, "Hansen vs. the World on the Greenhouse Threat," *Science*, June 2, 1989, pp. 1041–43.

[14]Ibid.

[15]Pamela Zurer, "EPA Urges Nations to Limit Greenhouse Gases, Protect Climate," *Chemical and Engineering News*, March 27, 1989, pp. 22–23.

[16]See Stephen H. Schneider, "The Greenhouse Effect: Science and Policy," *Science*, February 10, 1989, pp. 771–81.

[17]Quoted in Pamela Zurer, "Plan Now for Climate Change, Experts Say," *Chemical and Engineering News*, December 12, 1988, pp. 5–6.

Yet the nasty details of the greenhouse effect remain. Why is there no clear evidence that the sea level is rising at an accelerated rate? Why do most knowledgeable private-sector meteorological scientists, such as Richard Lindzen, Sloan Professor of Meteorology at MIT and member of the National Academy of Sciences, refuse to state that the greenhouse effect is either here or probable in the near future? Why have nearly all greenhouse models projected greater warming than has occurred? Why do records of ocean temperatures that were collected by the British Meteorological Office over the past 100 years show little or no warming at all?[18] Indeed, MIT's Lindzen may say it best: the greenhouse "is the only subject in atmospheric science where a consensus view has been declared before the research has hardly begun."[19]

The *New York Times* of April 11, 1991, reported the release of a National Academy of Sciences study on global warming that noted an increase in the atmospheric concentrations of carbon dioxide, methane, and chlorofluorocarbons (CFCs). Those measured increases are widely accepted by the scientific community. The report went on to predict that without remedial action, greenhouse gas concentrations will continue to rise and that this rise could cause an increase in average global temperature of 1.8° to 9.0° Fahrenheit. It is also speculated that the increase in temperature could ultimately be twice as great. We believe these predictions to be unwarranted.

Nevertheless, the report did not recommend drastic remedies to prevent global warming. It advocated instead more efficient coal and natural gas–fired electric generation plants and greater use of natural gas in general. Natural gas is certainly one of the cleanest and most efficient of fuels, but greater use would increase atmospheric methane. The report also recommended development of a new generation of nuclear reactors along with improved nuclear waste management procedures. Finally, it recommended increased research into alternative energy sources. Those recommendations

[18]"Has the Globe Really Warmed?" *Technology Review*, November/December 1989, p. 80. Global temperature monitoring by satellite has also not shown any obvious warming trend. See Roy W. Spencer and John R. Christy, "Precise Monitoring of Global Temperature Trends from Satellites," *Science*, March 30, 1990, pp. 1558–62.

[19]Quoted in Richard A. Kerr, "Greenhouse Skeptic out in the Cold," *Science*, December 1, 1989, pp. 1118–19.

are easy to agree with, and many are recommended elsewhere in this book. We find the report to be quite sensible in spite of our lack of agreement with its speculations concerning future temperature trends.

A major reason that we do not agree with the National Academy of Sciences' report is that as the greenhouse models mature, the warming predicted tends to lessen. T. M. L. Wigley, reporting in *Nature*, has uncovered a somewhat unexpected relationship between sulfur dioxide and the greenhouse effect.[20] Sulfur dioxide, one of the prime targets of the lobby against acid rain, tends to oxidize into sulfate in the atmosphere and thus promotes condensation in clouds. Those additional water droplets in clouds help reflect heat upward and, therefore, have a cooling effect on the earth. Since a large percentage of sulfur dioxide comes from burning high-sulfur coal, success in eliminating sulfur dioxide emissions may mean an exacerbation of any greenhouse effect.

The omission of sulfur dioxide emissions from the models may account for some of the overprediction of warming, but more sophisticated models of ice clouds (which act quite different from water clouds) and of ocean currents surely account for some of the overprediction as well.[21] It is therefore not surprising that the entire enhanced greenhouse effect is being subjected to searching criticism by a growing segment of the scientific community.[22]

The eruption of Mount Pinatubo in the Philippines may well prove to be a source of frustration to the purveyors of disastrous global warming predictions. That eruption has been described as possibly the largest of the century, and it has been roughly estimated that the volcano will inject 15 million tons (plus or minus 5 million tons) of sulfur dioxide into the atmosphere. The sulfur dioxide is converted into aerosol droplets of sulfuric acid that may remain in the atmosphere for as long as three years. The sulfuric acid aerosols have a net cooling effect since they tend to reflect solar radiation away from the earth. Pinatubo may have an average

---

[20]T. M. L. Wigley, "Possible Climate Change Due to Dioxide Derived Cloud Condensation Nuclei," *Nature*, June 1, 1989, pp. 365–67.

[21]Tim Beardsley, "Not So Hot: New Studies Question Estimates of Global Warming," *Scientific American*, November 1989, pp. 17–18.

[22]See, for example, the letters of R. S. Lindzen (MIT), W. A. Nierenberg (Scripps), R. Jastrow (Dartmouth), and others in *Science*, Janurary 5, 1990, pp. 14–15.

cooling effect of as much as 0.5° Celsius, or as much as the purported greenhouse warming of the past century.[23]

Is There Some Other Issue?

Perhaps the only good to come out of the controversy will accrue to those who study the phenomenon, because federal funding for research on global climate change is slated to increase dramatically over the near term.[24] That increase seems to prove that one way to acquire additional research funding is to garner media attention regardless of any necessary compromise in scientific rigor. As Stephen Schneider, one of the most avid and prolific proponents of global warming, puts it:

> On the one hand, as scientists, we are ethically bound to the scientific method, in effect promising to tell the truth, the whole truth, and nothing but—which means that we must include all the doubts, the caveats, the ifs, ands, and buts. On the other hand, we are not just scientists but human beings as well. And like most people we'd like to see the world a better place, which in this context translates into our working to reduce the risk of potentially disastrous climate change. To do that we need to get some broad-based support, to capture the public's imagination. That, of course, entails getting loads of media coverage. So we have to offer up scary scenarios, make simplified, dramatic statements and make little mention of the doubts that we may have.[25]

In every respect, that attitude betrays the trust that the American public places in the integrity of the scientific community. Any attempt by public policymakers to "do something" about a false or even benign greenhouse effect could be one of the most expensive errors ever made, not only in monetary terms but perhaps also in lives. A proposal that is being bandied about to reduce carbon dioxide emissions by 20 percent by the year 2000 could, in and of

[23]Richard A. Kerr, "Huge Eruption May Cool the Globe," *Science*, June 28, 1991, p. 1780.

[24]From $133.9 million in 1989 to an estimated $664 million in 1990. See Elisabeth Pennisi, "1990 Budget Preserves Healthy Increase for Global Climate Change Research," *The Scientist*, January 8, 1990, p. 2.

[25]Quoted in Jonathan Schell, "Our Fragile Earth," *Discover*, October 1989, pp. 45–50.

itself, cost the American economy trillions of dollars.[26] But perhaps worse, people who advocate some global commitment to make drastic cuts in carbon dioxide emissions need to understand that such a commitment must deny less developed countries the simple technology based on resources such as coal that would enhance the life expectancy of many people. Further, as Peter Passell has reported, some cost studies indicate that even if the greenhouse effect occurs, the cost of dealing with it may be much less expensive than attempting to prevent it today.[27] Those cost models are, of course, quite crude and speculative, but no more so than the greenhouse models themselves.

A call for doing something about the greenhouse effect is nothing less then a call for a permanent change in the economic infrastructure of the world.[28] Yet that call is based not only on the idea that the earth must grow warmer, but also on the idea that any warming will be detrimental to mankind rather than providing benefits such as a longer growing season. The evidence that both warming and any harmful effects from warming will occur in the foreseeable future is ludicrously small given the attention and money being lavished on the issue. One thing is clear, however: the prevention of any possible greenhouse effect will require a degree of bureaucratic control over economic affairs previously unknown in the West. Even Roger Revelle, the father of modern greenhouse science and source of Gore's concern over the issue (as expressed in *Earth in the Balance*), published a paper before his death which concluded that the warming was "too uncertain to justify drastic action at this time."[29]

Of course, the prospect for such control is clearly an enticement to people who advocate the prevention of global warming. Having been defeated at every turn in their quest to improve the condition of mankind by control of the distribution of income and wealth, the old guard of socialists and economic planners has formed itself into a new group of eco-socialists that has now an almost perfect

[26]Peter Passell, "Curing Greenhouse Effect Could Run into Trillions," *New York Times*, November 19, 1989, p.1.

[27]Ibid.

[28]See Schneider.

[29]S. Fred Singer, Roger Revelle, and Chauncey Starr, "What To Do about Greenhouse Warming: Look before You Leap," *Cosmos*, 1991, p. 28.

excuse for a new kind of social control: the economy can be blamed for every conceivable quirk in the weather. This aspect of global warming terrifies free-market advocates, and it is around this issue that the battle lines must be drawn. There is a greater probability that the future will be made worse by controls that are theoretically designed to prevent global warming than by any warming as such, because the controls will reduce growth and restrict freedom. That is the single genuine issue of the greenhouse effect, and it is not being communicated to the American people.

7. The Missing-Ozone Controversy

In 1974, M. J. Molina and F. S. Rowland, two scientists from the University of California, Irvine, published a paper in the prestigious journal *Nature* in which they postulated a threat to stratospheric ozone, which protects living things from ultraviolet radiation.[1] By use of theoretical calculations and models, Molina and Rowland proposed that chlorofluorocarbons (CFCs), which are chemical compounds of carbon, fluorine, and chlorine, might be the destructive agent. Since CFCs are nontoxic, highly stable, and widely used in refrigerators, air conditioners, and electronic cleaners, the charge had serious economic implications.

The Molina-Rowland claim was that the very stability of those compounds was the cause of their threat to stratospheric ozone. While CFCs remain stable indefinitely at relatively low altitudes, when carried into the stratosphere by updrafts of wind, they are able to absorb ultraviolet radiation and break down to release free chlorine. Since CFCs are about three times heavier than air, it takes a long time for them to reach the stratosphere, perhaps as many as 7 to 10 years. Once in the stratosphere, 12 to 25 miles above the earth's surface, their life expectancy drops to between 40 and 150 years, at which time their exposure to ultraviolet radiation causes them to break down and release chlorine atoms.

An ozone molecule contains three oxygen atoms. When ozone reacts with chlorine, one of the oxygen atoms combines with the chlorine atom, leaving an ordinary two-atom oxygen molecule and a molecule of chlorine monoxide. Meanwhile, ultraviolet radiation is absorbed by the two-atom oxygen molecules, causing them to split into two separate oxygen atoms. One of these oxygen atoms can now react with the chlorine monoxide and remove the chlorine monoxide's oxygen atom to form a new two-atom oxygen molecule and a free chlorine atom. The newly freed chlorine atom can now

[1]M. J. Molina and F. S. Rowland, "Stratospheric Sink for Chlorofluorocarbons: Chlorine Atom Catalyzed Destruction of Ozone," *Nature*, June 28, 1974, pp. 810–12.

react with another ozone molecule and start the process all over again.

Because of the possibility of many such reactions, the Molina-Rowland paper pointed out that it was possible for a few CFC molecules to do a great deal of damage to the stratospheric ozone layer. The implication of this research was that since annual global emissions of CFCs had increased steadily from less than half a million kilograms in 1935 to over 400 million kilograms in the mid-1970s, it was highly possible that mankind was destroying the ozone belt.[2] The cost of that destruction could be calamitous for the earth's flora and fauna. For mankind, it could lead to epidemic increases in a form of skin cancer. The implication was clear— the economic advantage of CFCs did not outweigh the potential catastrophic costs of their use. The only prudent course was to ban their manufacture and use, and quickly, before more damage was done.

The case against CFCs seems compelling on its face: chlorine can be stripped off CFCs by ultraviolet light; chlorine can destroy ozone; under the right conditions, a relatively small amount of chlorine can destroy a relatively large amount of ozone. Nevertheless, in attempting to understand the ozone puzzle, several essentials of the argument must be kept firmly in mind: it is not CFCs but chlorine that attacks ozone; the conditions must be right for small amounts of chlorine to destroy large amounts of ozone; ozone levels may fluctuate for reasons entirely independent of the levels of chlorine in the stratosphere. If relatively large amounts of chlorine are injected into the atmosphere from natural sources, if the conditions in the stratosphere are not right for the reactions to take place, or if some other force causes ozone levels to change, then any harmful effects of CFCs may be so minimal as to pose little or no threat. As we shall see, because of these points, the argument that CFCs are destroying the ozone is woefully deficient. Indeed, the entire case remains altogether conjectural.

The Ozone Roller Coaster

Ozone levels and the stock market have at least one thing in common: they fluctuate, sometimes quite violently and for no

[2]For data on CFC emissions from 1935 to 1980, see United Nations–U.S. Environment Program, *Environmental Data Report*, 2d ed., 1989/90, p. 28.

apparent reason. While many people profess to understand both phenomena, the truth is they do not. In 1956, G. M. B. Dobson, the Oxford professor for whom the Dobson unit of ozone measurement is named, first reported that in September–October 1956 at Halley Bay, Antarctica, atmospheric ozone was at a lower level than expected in the early spring, but that it returned to normal in November. In 1985 a British group, again at Halley Bay, reported that beginning in 1975 short-lived declines in atmospheric ozone were observed in October, but the levels returned to normal in November. And in 1986 Mark R. Schoeber and Richard S. Stolarski of the NASA Goddard Space Flight Center in Greenbelt, Maryland, reported that the decrease in ozone levels in Antarctica each spring seemed to be compensated for by an increase in ozone levels at lower latitudes, so that the total amount of ozone from the pole to 44 degrees south latitude remained approximately constant from August through November.

Those reports are often taken to be empirical verification of man's destruction of the ozone. On the contrary, what those reports say is that ozone seems to vary seasonally at certain locations—which is no more alarming than a report that in Boston many flowers seem to die in October and are reborn in May.

The seasonal variations are obviously connected with how ozone is made and destroyed in nature. When high-energy ultraviolet light is absorbed by an ordinary two-atom oxygen molecule, the light has sufficient energy to split the normal oxygen molecule into two oxygen atoms, which can then form three-atom ozone. Ozone is, therefore, being continuously formed—its supply is not static. And since oxygen is thousands of times more abundant than CFCs, the formation of ozone would at the very least be expected to equal its destruction by chlorine monoxide. When ozone is broken down by ultraviolet radiation into two-atom oxygen, the ozone absorbs the ultraviolet radiation. Those reactions are not symmetric as far as energy is concerned: ordinary oxygen absorbs a higher frequency form of ultraviolet radiation (energy) than ozone does. However, since ultraviolet radiation is absorbed by ordinary oxygen, it is incorrect to imply that only ozone protects against ultraviolet radiation. The production of ozone varies with the amount of solar radiation, which itself undergoes tremendous fluctuations not only by season but also over the years because of sunspots and other natural variations in solar activity. Because of that variation, there is no clear indication that the total amount of ozone in the stratosphere has been reduced. Perhaps of greater importance, no convincing measurements show that more ultraviolet radiation is reaching the earth's surface because of any alleged ozone depletion. In fact, some measures seem to show a decline in ultraviolet radiation falling on the United States.[3]

The production of ozone also varies by geographic region; its production is most efficient in the tropics both because ozone breakdown is less rapid in warm temperatures and because abundant sunlight stimulates production. Therefore, in the absence of atmospheric circulation, we would expect ozone to be more abundant in tropical latitudes. Instead, ozone is actually more abundant at middle and high latitudes (closer to the poles). That great difference clearly indicates that ozone must circulate about the globe. To understand how that circulation occurs, it is helpful to view the atmosphere as though it were a fluid that circulated in patterns called "planetary waves."[4] Those waves, which are influenced by many factors including seasonality, are responsible for distributing ozone unevenly over the globe and tend to form vortexes (akin to whirlpools) near the poles.

Ozone concentrations differ markedly in the Northern and Southern hemispheres even though there is no appreciable difference in the chemistry operating between the two hemispheres. Again planetary wave dynamics can account for hemispheric differences. The South Pole and Antarctica are considerably colder than the Arctic region, and the stratospheric circulation around the South Pole (the polar vortex) is stronger than at the North Pole. Further, in the Southern Hemisphere, the circulation reaches only as far south as 60 degrees south latitude for most of the year. In addition to these differences, planetary waves tend to break down the Antarctic vortex in the spring and as the polar temperature rises, the temperature difference between the equator and the South Pole lessens.

[3]S. Fred Singer, "Environmental Strategies with Uncertain Science," *Regulation*, Winter 1990, p. 65–70.

[4]See Murry L. Salby and Rolando R. Garcia, "Dynamical Perturbations to the Ozone Layer," *Physics Today*, March 1990, pp. 38–46.

Both of those effects tend to allow ozone-rich air to replace ozone-poor air that has been trapped in the Antarctic vortex over the preceding winter.

That explanation of how planetary waves cause the seasonal ozone fluctuation is called the "Dynamic Theory," and it is held by many scientists who study the ozone question. The strongest evidence for the theory is the link between temperature and ozone levels: the lower the temperature, the lower the amount of ozone found in the Antarctic stratosphere. In fact, the correlation between the temperature level of the Antarctic and ozone levels is much more impressive than the correlation between ozone and CFCs, no doubt because low temperatures favor ozone destruction. Since 1980, the temperature of the Antarctic has dropped dramatically, exceeding record lows. The Southern Hemisphere's stratosphere cooled by more than 2° Celsius between 1980 and 1985, and over Antarctica the stratosphere has cooled by 2°–4° Celsius since 1980. Further, since the level of CFCs in the atmosphere has been growing steadily by as much as 5 percent a year recently, the ozone "hole" should have deepened—but it has not. For example, ozone levels were higher in 1986 and 1984 than in 1985.

Even more puzzling, it was discovered in 1987 that on one day (September 5, 1987) ozone levels fell about 10 percent over an area of some three million square kilometers in Antarctica. Chemical conditions simply do not change this rapidly, again indicating that some dynamic influence was perturbing the Antarctic stratosphere.[5] The oscillating pattern of ozone clearly argues for a dynamic rather than a chemical explanation of ozone activity. It also argues that there may very possibly have been ozone "holes" in the past and that there will be others in the future quite independent of what is done by man.[6]

Finally, volcanic eruptions can so disturb the stratosphere that they may lead to significant ozone destruction. That effect was evident after the El Chichon eruption in 1982, which injected large

[5]Richard S. Stolarski, "The Antarctic Ozone Hole," *Scientific American*, January 1988, p. 36.

[6]Stefi Weisburd, "The Ozone Hole, Dynamically Speaking," *Science News*, November 29, 1986, p. 344–46.

quantities of sulfur dioxide into the stratosphere.[7] The gas condenses with water to form aerosol droplets of sulfuric acid, which can then become catalytic sites for ozone destruction.[8] Indeed, since the lightest CFC weighs approximately three times more than air, it is quite a puzzle how updrafts are able to carry significant amounts of CFCs upward several miles into the sky. Indeed, if the fluctuations in ozone are chemically induced at all, it is surely easier to believe a volcanic emissions theory than one that relies on the deus ex machina of an updraft.

The high probability that natural occurrences, such as volcanic eruptions, produce effects on ozone that dwarf anything done by man is dramatically demonstrated by the recent eruption of Mount Pinatubo in the Philippines. Arlin Krueger of the Goddard Space Flight Center has called Pinatubo "possibly the largest eruption of this century."[9] It has been calculated that the eruption of El Chichon in Mexico in 1982 could have catalyzed the destruction of as much as 15 percent of the stratospheric ozone in the middle layers of the Northern Hemisphere, a very significant amount when compared to manmade declines of 5 percent per *decade* claimed by more zealous environmentalists. The eruption of Mount Pinatubo will probably dwarf that of El Chichon, demonstrating once again the insignificance of manmade changes on the chemistry of the atmosphere.

Recently, there has been a marked increase in stratospheric chlorine monoxide, the chemical that has been implicated as the prime suspect in ozone destruction. But in spite of what the media have implied, that increase was not caused by man, but rather by Mount Pinatubo's venting of large quantities of sulfuric and hydrochloric acid. The sulfuric acid aerosols catalyze a reaction that ties up ambient nitrogen oxides, thus preventing them from forming chlorine nitrate compounds; as a result, chlorine monoxide is kept from forming. It is worth remembering that about 20 years ago some of our more zealous environmentalists helped to derail the supersonic transport project with the charge that the airplanes would emit

---

[7]R. L. Jones, "Depletion on Volcanic Aerosols," *Nature*, July 27, 1989, p. 269.

[8]Ibid.

[9]Quoted in Richard A. Kerr, "Huge Eruption May Cool the Globe," *Science*, June 28, 1991, p. 1780.

nitrogen oxide in their exhaust, which would in turn destroy the ozone and lead to increased skin cancer. The newly found benefits of nitrogen oxides in preventing the formation of chlorine monoxide are somewhat ironic.[10]

Many other chemicals may interact with CFCs to prevent conditions in the stratosphere from being as pristine as the theoretical arguments about CFC and ozone depletion presume. Methane, the feared "greenhouse gas" and the stuff of animal (and human) flatulence, inhibits the Molina-Rowland process, and chemicals such as bromine have been discovered that probably enhance the deleterious effects of CFCs on ozone.[11] Of course, none of these effects, or much of anything else in atmospheric chemistry, can be specified with any degree of precision.

Timothy Minton et al. have recently reported on their study of the mechanism by which chlorine monoxide reacts in a series of steps to liberate free chlorine, which is directly responsible for the breakdown of polar ozone. Their experimental results indicate the possibility that there could be two pathways for this reaction instead of the single pathway on which are based all calculations of the amount of ozone destroyed by chlorine. The significance of this finding is that far less ozone may be destroyed by chlorine than the single-pathway models predict.[12]

Given the tremendous variety of things that can cause natural fluctuation in stratospheric ozone, it is not at all surprising that variations in the quantity of ozone were observed by Dobson as far back as the 1950s, when CFC emissions were less than a tenth what they are today. Indeed, this fact alone calls into question the entire theory that ozone fluctuations are caused by CFCs, and we have no reason not to believe that ozone "holes" existed even in prehistoric times.

Still, the CFC theory does have something in common with many of the alleged modern causes of environmental "disaster": its relative importance has declined over time. In 1980 the National Academy of Sciences estimated that the maximum possible reduction

[10]See Richard A. Kerr, "New Assaults Seen on Earth's Ozone Shield," *Science* (February 14, 1992): 797–98.

[11]Michael B. McElroy et al., Reductions of Antarctic Ozone Due to Synergistic Interactions of Chlorine and Bromine," *Nature*, June 19, 1986, pp. 759–62.

[12]Timothy K. Minton et al., "Direct Observation of ClO from Chlorine Nitrate Photolysis," *Science*, November 20, 1992, p. 1342.

of stratospheric ozone by CFCs was 18 percent; over the years that maximum has been reduced to between 2 and 4 percent.[13] One would think that this reduction would be given prominent media attention, but it has not.

Effects of Ozone Fluctuations

Is there any evidence that the extra ultraviolet radiation associated with the ozone "hole" has damaged Antarctic marine life? Osmond Holm-Hansen of the Scripps Institute of Oceanography has studied the effect of Antarctic ozone depletion on phytoplankton, tiny plants at the base of the food chain. He has found that the increased radiation has had no significant effect on it or on the rest of the ecosystem.

However, the effect of ozone depletion on phytoplankton is certainly not yet a closed issue. In a study widely reported by the press, a team headed by a scientist from the University of California, Santa Barbara, estimated that as much as 2–4 percent of phytoplankton could be lost during periods of peak ozone depletion.[14] The press did not report the extreme measurement problems associated with this study. For example, the ozone layer varied severely almost day to day; at any one spot, it varied from more than 350 Dobson units, the approximate maximum in the Antarctic any time of the year, down to about 150 Dobson units. Within a day it could rebound to 350 Dobson units again. Furthermore, the natural variation in the phytoplankton population during the study was plus or minus 25 percent, which dwarfs the claimed ozone-induced variation of 2–4 percent and calls into question the significance of the study's statistical findings.

There has been little evidence of the ozone "hole" spreading to portions of the globe inhabited by people. Even if such a spread should occur, it would most likely happen in colder parts of the year, when there is little outdoor activity and when people wear more clothing. It is also ironic that nature, not mankind, has arranged for there to be a comparatively thin cover of ozone in the tropics where it is most needed.

[13]S. Fred Singer, "Stratospheric Ozone," Heritage Foundation Backgrounder, April 19, 1990, pp. 14–15.

[14]R. C. Smith et al., "Ozone Depletion: Ultraviolet Radiation and Phytoplankton Biology in Antarctic Waters," *Science*, February 1, 1992, pp. 952–58.

Recent CFC Horror Stories

One piece of evidence that the ozone "hole" is spreading was publicized on April 5, 1991, in both the *New York Times* and the *Washington Post*. The *Times* announced that the ozone loss over the United States was twice as fast as predicted and noted that the "EPA chief" found the news to be both stunning and disturbing. The *Post* story stated that skin cancer deaths could double in 40 years. Both stories went on to state that at latitudes relevant to the United States, declines in the ozone layer measured in late fall, winter, and early spring amounted to 4.5–5 percent in the past decade. On the basis of this finding, it was predicted that over the next half-century, about 12 million Americans would develop skin cancer and more than 200,000 would die from it. Under previous assumptions, only 500,000 cases of skin cancer and 9,300 fatalities had been predicted.

The rule of thumb used by scientists who study this problem is that for every 1 percent decrease in the high altitude ozone shield, 2 percent more ultraviolet radiation will reach the ground.[15] The *Post* implied that the ozone-measuring satellite recorded the amount of ultraviolet radiation actually reaching the ground. It did not. The amount of radiation reaching the ground was extrapolated from the satellite results (satellites cannot measure directly what happens on the ground). As we have noted, ground-based observations have not shown any significant increases in ultraviolet radiation over the years it has been measured.

The Total Ozone Mapping Spectrometer (TOMS), which did the measuring, has been in orbit since 1979. Over the years its reflecting surface has been darkened because of traces of hydrocarbons and other materials in space. In the spring of 1991 the spectrometer was recalibrated to compensate for the loss of reflectivity. The recalibration was done using the best science available; however, recalibrating an instrument that has been in orbit for a dozen years is, at best, inexact. The fact that the announced change in ozone measurement coincides with the recalibration causes us to suspect the accuracy of the measurement. Moreover, NASA's increased

[15]We thank Dr. William Mankin, National Center for Atmospheric Research, Boulder, Colorado, for granting a telephone interview to Harold Lyons on July 19, 1991. Much of the factual material in this and the following paragraph was obtained from that interview. The interpretation of these facts is ours alone.

91

interest in ozone may have more to do with the agency's need for media exposure and its congressional funding difficulties than with any difficulties with the ozone.[16]

The fact that there has been no increase in ultraviolet radiation reaching the ground makes it difficult to ascribe any skin cancer to "ozone depletion." The incidence of malignant melanoma, the most virulent form of skin cancer, seems to have been increasing since 1935, well before the widespread use of CFCs. As for the milder form of skin cancer, one could probably make a better case for a correlation between the meagerness of sunbathing apparel and the incidence of skin cancer than for any correlation between skin cancer and CFCs.

Replacing CFCs

Nevertheless, concern about CFCs led to their ban as aerosol propellants in 1978. The ban caused no great economic or convenience hardship since plenty of satisfactory substitutes were available. Only after discovery of the "hole" in 1985 did pressure to completely eliminate CFCs result in international agreements (such as the Montreal Protocol) to cut the use of CFCs at least in half by 1999. (The EPA, however, has decided to stop all U.S. production of CFCs by the end of 1995.) Those agreements were made before scientific research could establish how much the compounds contributed to what might well be a preponderantly natural event. Again, as in the case of the greenhouse effect, the cost to the public of rushing to correct a problem that may not exist is great. In fact, the rush to fix the ozone "hole" may lead to corrective measures that are themselves a greater health hazard than any conceivable ozone problem.

The compounds currently being considered as interim substitutes for CFCs will be less effective and will require the redesign of practically every piece of equipment now using CFCs. The DuPont Company, one of the principal manufacturers of CFCs, has stated that the compounds are used by 5,000 businesses in over a third of a million locations to produce goods and services worth more than $28 billion a year in the United States alone. Further, CFC-related jobs total over three-quarters of a million, and more than

---

[16]See "Press-Release Ozone Hole," *Wall Street Journal*, February 28, 1992, p. A14.

$135 billion of installed equipment in the United States depends on CFCs, as does 75 percent of the U.S. food supply.[17] When one considers all the refrigeration equipment, air conditioners (automobile, home, and commercial), and other equipment that will have to be radically modified or replaced, the size of the cost is evident.

Commercial air conditioning and refrigerating units generally have a life span of 20 to 40 years, so simply allowing the existing capital stock to be replaced when it wears out is not to be allowed under present agreements. Robert Watson of NASA has been quoted as saying that when CFCs are banned, more people will probably die from food poisoning caused by inadequate refrigeration than from ozone depletion attributable to CFCs.[18] Further, since most of the promising CFC substitutes are less efficient, the result of removing CFCs may well be an increase in atmospheric pollution due to greater fuel use. There may also be an increased fire hazard since some of the proposed substitutes are flammable.[19]

Moreover, the *Wall Street Journal* on July 7, 1991, reported that the much-heralded substitutes for CFCs had been shown to be toxic. The compounds have produced nonmalignant tumors in the pancreas and testes of male rats. Again the report reinforces our argument that it will be extremely difficult to find substances that have the unique physical and chemical properties of CFCs without toxicity. The *Journal* article quoted Jerry Kestenbaum, vice president of Refrigeration Sales Company of Long Island City, New York, who felt that even if some entirely new substance were invented today, CFCs probably could not be replaced until 1996. Allied Signal, which had been testing the new alternatives to CFCs, announced that it had suspended plans to market them. A spokesman for the Carrier Company also announced the suspension of sales of new industrial chillers that use the new CFC substitutes.

For the record, DuPont is not only the major manufacturer of CFCs; it is also the only sizable firm with plausible substitutes. DuPont has apparently invested more than $170 million in research and capital for the creation of interim substitutes and apparently

---

[17]"Protecting the Ozone Layer, The Search for Solutions" (Wilmington, Del.: E.I. DuPont Co., 1989).

[18]Jane S. Shaw and Richard L. Stroup, "Can Consumers Save the Environment?" *Consumer's Research*, September 1990, pp. 11–15.

[19]Our auto mechanic reports that propane works!

plans to spend $1 billion during the next decade. Not surprisingly, the company wants a complete phaseout of CFCs in developed countries by the year 2000. In testimony before the U.S. House of Representatives, a DuPont representative bemoaned the fact that several CFC plants have been opened in less developed countries since the Montreal Protocol.[20] We wonder how much of DuPont's concern over CFCs is driven by the likelihood that the company may be the sole supplier of any substitute for years to come.

The Missing Controversy

It would seem fair to state that most students of the ozone issue differ in the emphasis they place on the chemical (CFC) and the dynamic explanations.[21] But even here, evolving research indicates that the two theories may interact in very complicated ways. For example, sunspot activity may not only drive weather patterns but also may be directly linked to ozone formation and destruction.[22] In fact, a relationship between total ozone and sunspot activity was noted as far back as 1910 with the work of W. J. Humphreys. But this controversy has never been allowed to surface in the popular media, and most people, even those who are highly informed on environmental matters, do not know that alternative explanations exist.

In our view, all this uncertainty justifies a prudent delay of action until further research can bring the ozone matter closer to scientific resolution. The findings to date form an interesting scientific puzzle but surely not the warning of environmental disaster that has been sounded. Yet the environmental lobby insists that a proven non-toxic chemical be replaced with chemicals of unknown virtue and at enormous cost to the economy. It is absolutely astonishing to us that the urgency of such action not only remains undemonstrated but also virtually undebated.

---

[20]A. Dwight Bedsole, "Oral Testimony," U.S. House of Representatives Committee on Energy and Commerce, January 25, 1990.

[21]Richard A. Kerr, "Winds, Pollutants Drive Ozone Hole," *Science*, October 9, 1987, pp. 156–58.

[22]Richard A. Kerr, "Sunspot-Weather Link Holding Up," *Science*, November 25, 1988, pp. 1124–25.

8. Acid Rain

Reports from such "blue ribbon" groups as President Jimmy Carter's Council on Environmental Quality, books such as Robert Ostmann's *Acid Rain: A Plague upon the Waters*,[1] and a seemingly unending series of television accounts have convinced many Americans that acid rain is a grave environmental problem. What is almost never aired is the sincere scientific disagreement over whether acid rain is much of a problem at all, not to mention the growing number of scientists and economists who question the payoff from large spending schemes designed to reduce acid rain, such as the Clean Air Amendments of 1990.

How Much Acid Do We Allow?

The accepted scientific measure of acidity or alkalinity is the pH scale, which is calibrated from a low of 0 to a high of 14. A neutral substance (neither acidic nor basic) registers 7 on the scale, and a pH of 0 indicates a substance which is highly acid. Conversely, a pH measure of 14 indicates a substance that is highly basic. The scale is constructed so that a change of one point of pH represents a 10-fold change in acidity or alkalinity; a pH of 6 is 10 times more acidic then a pH of 7. The pH of pure water is 7, the pH of lemon juice is about 2, and the pH of human stomach juices is between 1 and 2. Rainfall is naturally acidic, largely because of the carbon dioxide in the air; CO_2 combines with water vapor to produce carbonic acid. Rain that fell before the industrial age is generally estimated to have had an average pH of between 5.6 and 5.0, depending on the location.[2] This natural range of pH levels is quite

---

[1]Robert Ostmann, *Acid Rain: A Plague upon the Waters* (Minneapolis: Dillon Press, 1982).

[2]See J. Laurence Kulp, "Acid Rain: Causes, Effects, and Control," *Regulation*, Winter 1990, pp. 41–50, and Edward C. Krug and Charles R. Frink, "Acid Rain on Acid Soil: A New Perspective," *Science*, August 5, 1983, pp. 520–25.

critical because most species of sports fish do not survive well in water with a pH of less than about 5.0.

Rain that has a pH lower than the natural level is called acid rain and it has been known to have a pH close to 4.0. But even this definition of acid rain must be interpreted with care because the acidity of rainfall depends on location. Some locations have more natural acidic elements in the air than others. It is fairly well understood that a major cause of excess acidity in rain comes from the reaction of sulfur dioxide with water and oxygen in the atmosphere, which leads to the creation of sulfuric acid. Nitric acid is also usually found in acid rain, but it is often thought to be beneficial in that it provides fertilizer (nitrogen) for plants.[3] Therefore, sulfur dioxide emissions from electric generating plants, heating, industrial processes, and other sources are major targets in acid rain reduction programs. However, manmade sulfur dioxide emissions have been on a steady decline in the United States since the mid-to late-1970s. Those emissions are now estimated to be about the same as in 1930.[4]

The problems of acid rain, like most ecological issues, involve measurement and perception of costs and benefits. Does an incremental increase in the acidity of rainwater make any difference given that rain is naturally acidic? What are the costs and benefits of reducing the acidity in rainwater to natural levels?

How Long Have These Lakes Been Dead?

The most common ecological alarm over acid rain is that it is destroying forests and creating "dead" lakes devoid of fish. Other alleged harmful effects are the retardation of crop growth, the production of haze, the destruction of building materials, and the adverse health effects associated with breathing acidic air.

It may be true that acid rain contributes to haze, but it is difficult to get a scientific handle on how much haze is natural and how much is directly caused by excess acidity. Some changes in visibility are consistent with sulfur dioxide emission trends and some are not. On the other hand, the charge appears to be false that acid rain has any detrimental effects on agriculture at the levels of acidity

---

[3]Some students of acid rain feel that this acid may lead to excess fertilization, which might prevent trees from adjusting properly to freezing weather.

[4]Kulp.

now experienced or anticipated in agricultural regions.[5] In fact, acid rain provides additional fertilizer for free. Harm to the respiratory system or the eyes of human beings or animals has not been shown except at exposures many times greater than present levels.[6] Finally, the data at hand suggest it is unlikely that any significant shortening of the life of building materials can be associated with present levels of acid rain, although the life of marble is evidently shortened in urban areas where the acidity is related to the large number of automobiles and the burning of large quantities of high-sulfur coal.[7]

As for damage to forests, the only large-scale study of the alleged problem failed to confirm the environmentalists' fears. The National Acid Precipitation Assessment Program (NAPAP) was funded by Congress in 1980 as a 10-year research effort. It was one of the largest scientific endeavors ever undertaken, costing nearly $400 million and involving thousands of scientists from government agencies, private industrial and research firms, and universities. No other study on acid rain can rival this one in scope and magnitude. It states the following:

> Controlled exposure studies of simulated acidic deposition on seedlings have not detected injury or other adverse effects on the foliage of conifer and hardwood species tested down to a pH of 3.5. . . . The average annual pH of rainfall in the United States rarely falls below pH 4.1.[8]

Those findings are certainly at odds with the more popular accounts of forest devastation that have appeared in *Newsweek*, *National Parks*, *UNESCO Courier*, and hundreds if not thousands of

---

[5]National Acid Precipitation Assessment Program (NAPAP), *Interim Assessment: The Causes and Effects of Acidic Deposition*, vol. 1 (Washington: U.S. Government Printing Office, 1987).

[6]The literature on the lack of health damage from acid rain (including possible damage from swimming in acid lakes) is reviewed in Melvin A. Benarde, *Our Precarious Habitat: Fifteen Years Later* (New York: John Wiley and Sons, 1989). See also Dixy Lee Ray, *Trashing the Planet: How Science Can Help Us Deal with Acid Rain, Depletion of the Ozone, and Nuclear Waste (Among Other Things)* (Washington: Regnery Gateway, 1990).

[7]Kulp.

[8]NAPAP, 1–28.

other media presentations.[9] Unlike many studies of forest decline that are largely anecdotal in nature, the NAPAP report is a systematic and comprehensive study of acid rain. It also has the great virtue of agreeing with common sense. Any profound effect on forests or other growing things should be obvious, especially to city dwellers. The acidity of some Los Angeles fogs measures less than 3 on the pH scale, and the only forests known to be declining because of pollution are in the Los Angeles air basin and the southern Sierra Nevada. (Even those declines may end up being attributable more to ozone pollution than to acid rain.[10]) The fact that similar effects are not seen elsewhere should raise questions about acid rain's consequences.

The environmentalists' original charge that acid rain is killing our forests has now been moderated to a charge that it is a "stress factor," like hard winters or drought, that *may* contribute to forest damage. Apparently, when people have a mindset that economic activity kills trees, it is difficult to persuade them otherwise, no matter how extensive the evidence. Trees die, and natural dieback is a phenomenon that is by no means new.[11] However, it is difficult to refute a stress or multiple stress theory of forest decline because such a theory is far too vague to offer a testable scientific hypothesis. A report in *Nature* put it well:

> The concept of multiple stress was initially tempting, as it is vague enough to apply to any damage which cannot be explained in any other way. Its very versatility, however, makes it impossible to test and useless to those looking for the causes and mechanisms of forest damage.[12]

Moreover, a study done between 1971 and 1990 by the Finnish Forest Research Institute found no decline in European forests. The study estimated that the "growing stock and forest growth in

[9]See "Rediscovering Planet Earth," *U.S. News and World Report*, October 31, 1988, pp. 56–61; "Planet at the Crossroads," *National Parks*, March/April 1990, pp. 25–43; and "The Fragile Forest," *UNESCO Courier*, January 1989, pp. 13–17.

[10]NAPAP, I-28.

[11]See Dieter Mueller-Dombois, "Natural Dieback in Forests," *Bioscience*, September 1987, pp. 575–83.

[12]L. W. Blank et al., "New Perspectives on Forest Decline," *Nature*, November 1988, pp. 27–30.

Europe increased between 1971 and 1990 by 25 and 30 percent respectively."[13]

In summary, several hundred million dollars worth of research done by thousands of scientists in the United States and Europe has not been able to show that acid rain is doing any significant harm to forests. Yet the accusation that acid rain is destroying our forests continues. An acquaintance of ours who recently visited Mt. Mitchell in North Carolina was told by a U.S. forest ranger that a stand of dead trees was the result of acid rain. But according to a member of the Spruce-Fir Research Cooperative of the Forest Service, the trees are actually believed to have been killed by the balsam woolly adelgid.[14] Our friend did not seem to feel any better when we told her of this alternative explanation. Despite the reluctance to assign any forest death to natural causes, there is a growing literature that explains dieback in forests in just those terms. The literature rejects alarmist predictions that "new types" of forest damage would lead to *Waldsterben* (forest death).[15]

What of the charge that acid rain kills our lakes? Therein lies one of the most interesting and neglected tales of all. In a brilliant paper published in *Science* almost a decade ago, Edward Krug and Charles Frink wondered whether ordinary rainfall landing on acid soil might be causing some lakes to acidify.[16] To understand their argument, amateur gardeners need only recall that acid-loving plants such as azaleas thrive when they are mulched with pine needles or peat moss, both of which leach acid into the soil. The floor of a forest can become so acidic when covered with humus and mosses that ordinary water can take up a good deal of acidity when it runs off. For most lakes, the run-off from surrounding land is a much greater source of new water than is the rain that falls directly into the lake, and rain water is less acidic than the ground on which it falls.[17] Moreover as a forest ages, the acidic layer builds on the floor. This build-up not only imparts acidity to water, but also tends

[13]Pekka E. Kauppi et al., "Biomass and Carbon Budget of European Forests, 1971 to 1990," *Science*, April 3, 1992, p. 73.

[14]See Mary Beth Adams, "Can't See the Forest for the Trees," *Policy Review*, Summer 1990, p. 83.

[15]Blank; also, Dieter Muller-Dombois.

[16]Krug and Frink.

[17]Ibid, p. 521.

to hold water longer, allowing the acidity to increase more than if the water ran off more quickly.

But why have the fish died? Is it not true that when Teddy Roosevelt fished in Lake Colden, it was one of the most productive trout lakes in the eastern United States, and that now it is nearly fishless? True enough, but the fish in Roosevelt's day might have been produced by what we would now call an ecological disaster: the clear-cutting and burning of forests in the last century. Slash-and-burn logging leaves the forest floor in ashes, and subsequent rain running over those ashes becomes very basic (grandmother ran water through ashes to make lye). The basic run-off, in turn, could have made the lakes basic enough to allow fish to thrive until the forest once again matured and produced an acidic floor and the associated acid run-off.

Krug and Frink cite discoveries of this reforestation effect (cutting and regrowing of trees) on acidity in Norway and elsewhere. Core samples taken from the bottom of lakes have verified that many "dead" lakes were always dead except for a short interval when heavy logging was being done nearby. For example, Kejimkujik Lake in Nova Scotia had a pH of 4.0 in 1850, rose to a pH of 5.0 with the cutting and burning of its watershed, and now has reacidified to a pH of 4.8. Lake Langtjern in Norway was more acidic 800 years ago than today. Areas of Australia, New Zealand, and Florida are replete with acidic bodies of water even though little or no acid rain falls on them. A University of New Hampshire study of ice core samples from the Antarctic and Himalaya mountains found samples as old as 350 years high in acid.[18] Numerous other examples, including lakes in the Adirondacks, can be found.[19]

The hypothesis about the acidity of run-off helps to explain a great many anomalies in the "acid lake" phenomenon. Why, for example, can lakes of similar size in virtually the same location vary greatly in acidity? The differences can usually be accounted for by differences in land use and differences in the alkalinity of the bedrock contiguous to the lakes.

As expected, avid environmentalists discount Krug and Frink's account. That account not only fails to blame present economic

[18]Benarde.

[19]Edward C. Krug, "Fish Story: The Great Acid Rain Flimflam," *Policy Review*, Spring 1990, pp. 44–8.

activity for the problem but it also finds some saving grace in an environmentally deplored method of timber harvest.[20] Even without the Krug and Frink explanation, people should be calmed by the fact that with the decline of sulfur emissions, acid rain should diminish. Indeed, any acidity problem would be even smaller had the 1970 Clean Air Act not required the removal of fly ash along with sulfur: fly ash is basic and helps to neutralize sulfuric acid.

Whichever explanation of acid lakes one believes, the number of lakes affected is very small. In the Adirondacks, where much of the complaint is centered, NAPAP estimated that only around 2 percent of the lakes have a pH below 5. In the Northeast the NAPAP estimate of such lakes is around 1 percent. None were found in the upper Midwest, southern Blue Ridge, or mountainous West.

Perhaps We Should Have Done Nothing

What then is the cost of acid rain? At a symposium in 1984, Thomas Crocker, citing a University of Wyoming study done for the EPA, estimated a cost of around $5 billion for 1978 in the eastern third of the United States, a figure often referred to in the press.[21] But in the discussion of this estimate, Paul MacAvoy, a distinguished economist and then dean of the Graduate School of Management at the University of Rochester commented that "the $5 billion estimate is not reproducible . . . [and is] . . . purely a judgmental number derived from the author's own experience and imagination." MacAvoy conjectured that research on the harm from acid rain was not being done because such research would show that a large-scale program to reduce acid rain was not justified.[22] Apparently taken aback by MacAvoy's challenge, Crocker replied,

---

[20] An example of citing some of those studies while discounting them can be found in various popular accounts of the evils of acid rain. For example, see Volker A. Mohnen, "The Challenge of Acid Rain," *Scientific American*, August 1988, pp. 30–38.

[21] Thomas D. Crocker, "Estimates of Acid Deposition Control Benefits: A Bayesian Perspective," in *Conference on Acid Rain*, ed. by Paulette Mandelbaum (New York: Plenum Press, 1984), pp. 77–93. This figure is also sometimes referred to by those who are not particularly sympathetic to the claims of harm by acid rain. See Benarde, p. 410.

[22]Paul W. MacAvoy, "Response to Thomas D. Crocker," in Mandelbaum, pp. 99–101.

"Frankly, I disagree only a little with respect to Paul's comments."[23] In contrast, the director of research for the NAPAP report, J. Lawrence Kulp, puts the total benefit to the country of eliminating acid rain at around $100 million—about the cost of a single large stack scrubber for an electric utility company.[24]

There have also been attempts to measure the benefits of emission control in lives saved, but Robert Crandall and many other economists point out that those estimates never seem to include the deaths that might be caused by loss of income from such draconian controls.[25] The effects of income on health are nonlinear; an incremental increase in income for a poor person is associated with a greater improvement in health than the same increase for a rich person. Could it be that the number of lives saved from emission control might be less than the number lost because of reduced incomes for the poor? Indeed, we might ask why environmentalists overlook this obvious problem, since it is quite likely that any attempt to return all rain to its preindustrial pH would result in more deaths than doing nothing at all.

Finally, acidic lakes are not necessarily undesirable for human use. Swimmers prefer the algae- and leech-free clear waters of acidic lakes such as Lake Colden, and some of the acidic lakes on Cape Cod National Seashore are quite popular.[26] No eye damage has been found from swimming in those waters.[27] (Incidentally, the reflective properties of sulfur dioxide in clouds help to cool the earth—which should be of comfort to believers in global warming.)

Acidic lakes can be converted relatively inexpensively into basic lakes by simply liming their watersheds. Every acidic lake in the country could thus be neutralized for a few hundred thousand dollars a year. Liming has been resisted by some environmentalists because it would kill sphagnum moss at the bottom of lakes. As we have pointed out elsewhere, pleasing environmentalists can be difficult.

The Clean Air Amendments of 1990 called for removing 10 million tons of sulfur dioxide from the air on top of the 8 million tons

---

[23]Ibid., discussion by Thomas Crocker, p. 103.

[24]Kulp, 47.

[25]Robert W. Crandall, "Response to C. Hoff Stauffer," in Mandelbaum, pp. 59–73.

[26]Krug, p. 48.

[27]See Benarde, p. 411ff.

already removed by the 1970 Clean Air Act. The difference is that, like most economic processes, removing an additional increment of sulfur dioxide will be enormously more costly than removing the first increment. S. Fred Singer, professor of environmental science at the University of Virginia, states that "the benefits of acid rain control are nowhere commensurate with the enormous costs about to be placed on the American consumer," a cost estimated to be over $100 billion over the next 20 years.[28]

Acid rain has been studied and deliberated on for over a decade at a taxpayer cost of hundreds of millions of dollars. The NAPAP report has been largely ignored because it does not reach the "right" conclusion. Indeed, according to *Science*, the major problem with the report is that it concentrated too much on science and not enough on politics.[29] Most unbiased observers believe that acid rain affects at most 10 percent of eastern lakes and streams, that it might contribute to the decline of red spruce, that it has some minor corrosion effect on buildings and materials, and that it may slightly impair visibility in the Northeast and parts of the West. The question is whether the correction of these effects is worth billions of dollars when some simple changes in environmental regulation (such as removing bureaucratic impediments to plant modernization) could produce the same level of sulfur dioxide in 20 years instead of the 10 years proposed by the new Clean Air Amendments. Since sulfur dioxide was diminishing under the old law, doing nothing at all might have been the wisest policy of all. But the new Clean Air Act Amendments, largely a product of the media and professional environmental agitators who prevented the American people from receiving the good news on acid rain, foreclosed such a sensible option.

[28]S. Fred Singer, "Clean Air Hype," *Policy Review*, Summer 1990, p. 85. The cost estimate is in J. Laurence Kulp, "No Acid Rain Crisis," *Policy Review*, Summer 1990, p. 82.

[29]See Leslie Roberts, "Learning from an Acid Rain Program," *Science*, March 15, 1991, pp. 1302–5.

9. The Safest Fuel

On the first floor of the French Army Museum in the Invalides in Paris stands an enormous stuffed armored black horse topped by an equally impressive black suit of knightly armor. Few people are able to stand before this deadly man-horse combination and not feel at least a little of the fear that it must have transmitted to any battlefield opponent. But another consideration comes to the mind of anybody who has thought much about nuclear energy: could this have been the "atomic bomb" of the Middle Ages? It surely had enormous relative power, but did the people fear the horse when it was not being used for war? Or were the French too smart for such confusion?

A moment's reflection on the West's progress in energy use will demonstrate that it has been a movement away from ecologically destructive, unsafe, and expensive fuels, toward clean, safe, and inexpensive ones: wood to coal to petroleum to uranium. The most dangerous common occupation in the United States is that of lumberjack,[1] and if the economy were fueled by wood, the ecological and human devastation would be unbelievable. Coal is better, but it still exacts a great toll in miner deaths and ecological destruction. Petroleum is an enormous improvement over coal and, as we hope to show, nuclear power is vastly superior to petroleum for generating electricity. The trouble with nuclear power is that, like the animal in the Parisian museum, it is easy to confuse the warhorse with the workhorse, especially with a little help from the media.

Nuclear Opposition

The atomic bomb and nuclear power were, of course, both invented in the United States in the mid-20th century. The early promise of nuclear power was the same as it is today: a cheap, safe, reliable, and clean alternative to fossil fuels. Yet after the

[1]From data compiled by J. Paul Leigh, San Jose State University, as reported in *USA Today*, January 6, 1989.

U.S. government spent large amounts of money subsidizing private industry's development and demonstration of nuclear power, the industry has virtually collapsed: not a single U.S. reactor has been ordered since 1978, and many that were started have been abandoned at an estimated cost to the operating companies of $10 billion–$25 billion. Several studies have concluded that the average price of electricity will rise 22–35 percent as increased completion costs for nuclear plants and the costs of abandonment are passed along to ratepayers.[2]

We know of no energy specialist who denies that nuclear power is the only viable alternative to fossil fuels given present technology. Other energy sources (solar, geothermal, wind, biomass, etc.) can supplement fossil fuels, but none can replace them on a large-scale commercial basis. Other nations, such as France, have adopted nuclear power to a much greater extent than the United States; and Japan, a country with the best of reasons to be nuclearphobic, announced in 1990 that it will turn to nuclear energy to alleviate its dependence on oil imports.

The opposition to nuclear power, which blossomed in the early 1970s, was led by groups with names such as Clamshell, Crabshell, and Cactus and by a group headed by Ralph Nader, Critical Mass. They were able to exploit the public's confusion of nuclear reactors with nuclear bombs and feed the fear that a reactor could explode, killing thousands and deforming thousands more. The fear is unfounded: a nuclear power plant cannot explode like a nuclear bomb. A nuclear bomb requires a very high percentage of uranium 235, far higher than the maximum of 3 percent found in a nuclear power plant. In addition, a bomb must be triggered by a special explosive device not found in a nuclear power plant.[3] Yet opponents of nuclear power continue to present the bomb analogy to the public although they must know that it is untrue.

The dire predictions of the "no nukes" protesters seemed to be validated on March 28, 1979, when an accident occurred at the Three Mile Island nuclear power plant near Harrisburg, Pennsylvania. A much more serious accident occurred at Chernobyl in the Soviet

[2]John L. Campbell, *Collapse of an Industry: Nuclear Power and the Contradictions of U.S. Policy* (Ithaca, N.Y.: Cornell University Press, 1988), pp. 3–4.

[3]Jesse S. Doolittle, *Energy: A Crisis, a Dilemma, or Just Another Problem*, 2d ed. (Cleveland: Matrix Publishers, 1982).

Union on April 26, 1986, and did much to further erode public confidence in nuclear plants, as did numerous television programs and movies implying massive meltdowns burning through the earth to China. Given those and other images, it is no wonder that nuclear power is viewed by many as the riskiest of undertakings.

Three Mile Island and Chernobyl

Nuclear fission is the splitting of an atom's nucleus; it results in the release of large amounts of heat energy. It is an understatement to say that the splitting is difficult to accomplish. The only element found in nature that is readily fissionable is uranium, and even then only a particular isotope (variation) of uranium, uranium 235, is suitable. About 99 percent of the naturally occurring uranium is in the form of another isotope, uranium 238, and less than seven-tenths of 1 percent is 235. Therefore, natural uranium must be enriched (that is, the concentration of uranium 235 must be increased to about 3 percent) before it can be used for nuclear fission. After enrichment the uranium is converted into small pellets that are packed into rods. Those rods are then bundled to become the core of a nuclear reactor.

The uranium 235 pellets emit neutrons that bump into surrounding uranium 235 atomic nuclei. The atomic-level bumping provides the force to split the nuclei and release the heat energy that drives the reactor. Only slow neutrons travel at the right speed to do this work, and they must be slowed down by the reactor itself, using water, beryllium, or graphite—substances called moderators. If the neutrons are blocked completely from bumping into adjacent nuclei, there can be no fission at all. Thus the speed of the fission reaction can be controlled by blocking the neutrons. The blocking is done by inserting something between the uranium rods, such as control rods of boron steel or cadmium, which capture the neutrons. Pushing control rods into the core of the reactor slows the fission and the release of heat; pulling them out speeds up the process and increases the generation of heat.

If this entire package of uranium and control rods is surrounded by something like water, which can transfer the heat to an electric turbine, it constitutes a nuclear electric power plant. Three Mile Island used what is known as a pressurized water reactor system, which places water under pressure of up to 2,500 pounds per square inch (so that its boiling point is raised). The water was pumped through the reactor and then to a heat exchanger where it generated steam to drive electric turbines. The March 1979 accident was caused by the failure of a water pump, followed by operator errors in controlling the emergency cooling of the reactor. The pump failure caused water, which acted both as a coolant and as a moderator, to be cut off from the core of the reactor. The loss of the water moderator stopped the nuclear reaction because there was nothing to slow the neutrons. However, the continued heat build up without the water coolant was enough to cause a partial meltdown of the core. Operator error prevented the timely provision of available emergency cooling, converting a minor difficulty into a major problem.

For several weeks after the accident, the media issued sensational and conflicting reports concerning the release of radioactive materials into the atmosphere. Those reports tended to cause near panic in the vicinity of the plant. In fact, no significant radioactive material leaked into the atmosphere because a containment shell surrounded the reactor, and it contained both the radioactivity and nearly a million gallons of low-level radioactively contaminated water.[4] The shell was made of several feet of reinforced concrete plus a steel casing, a design typical of U.S. nuclear reactors. Early reports, for example, of significant radioactive iodine leakage were false.[5] It was later estimated that the total whole-body dose of alpha radiation downwind of the plant was 0.004 percent of the annual dose from natural sources.[6] Nobody was killed or suffered any measurable physical harm. Six years after the incident, a study by the Commonwealth of Pennsylvania detected no increase in cancer incidence within a 20-mile radius of the plant.[7]

As a result of the Three Mile Island incident, major and badly needed changes were made in the operation of nuclear plants.

[4]William Booth, "Post Mortem on Three Mile Island," *Science*, December 4, 1987, pp. 1342–45.

[5]F. R. Mynatt, "Nuclear Reactor Safety Research since Three Mile Island," *Science*, April 9, 1982, pp. 131–5.

[6]David M. Gates, *Energy and Ecology* (Sunderland, Mass.: Sinauer Associates, 1985), p. 322.

[7]Melvin A. Benarde, *Our Precarious Habitat: Fifteen Years Later* (New York: John Wiley and Sons, 1989), p. 365.

These included additional instrumentation and computerized safe-guards, better qualified operators, and increased simulator training for operators. Three Mile Island was the most serious nuclear accident that has ever happened in the United States, and yet it was not a disaster either for people or for the ecology. How strange that the American people still view Three Mile Island as a disaster rather than as proof that American reactors are constructed to prevent catastrophe.

A far more serious accident occurred at Chernobyl in the Soviet Union in 1986. The accident resulted in 31 fatalities, some 200 people being so severely hurt that their outlook is still in doubt, the evacuation of 135,000 people from the area, and the release of large amounts of radioactive material into the atmosphere. The Chernobyl reactor differed markedly from the Three Mile Island reactor in that the neutrons were moderated (slowed) by graphite instead of water. Perhaps more serious, the Chernobyl reactor had no containment shell.

Chernobyl's graphite moderator system did not have the fail-safe property of the Three Mile Island reactor. In the United States if water is cut off, the fission reaction stops because the moderator (water) is removed. With the Chernobyl reactor, water was used as a coolant and, along with graphite, as a partial moderator. When the reactor's core is deprived of water, the graphite continues to act as a moderator so the fission does not necessarily stop.[8] Worse, with the coolant removed, the reactor may actually speed up. The reactor does not go to critical mass like a nuclear bomb, but it can blow itself apart because of chemical reactions (such as steam being generated when water falls on hot metal).

But there was another serious problem at Chernobyl that was perhaps more important than the physical design of the reactor—operator failure. The accident happened during an experiment to see if back up systems would operate when the reactor was cut off from external power supplies. Through an almost unbelievable sequence of events in which the staff violated safety rules and deliberately disabled safety systems, the reactor speeded up out of control, fuel overheated, fuel rods began to rupture, coolant turned

[8]Charles H. Atwood, "Chernobyl—What Happened?" *Journal of Chemical Education*, December 1988, pp. 1037–41. See also John F. Ahearne, "Nuclear Power after Chernobyl," *Science*, May 8, 1987, pp. 673–79.

into steam, and the resulting pressure was so great that it blew the reactor lid off. Hot pieces of reactor core went flying, and a number of fires were started. The accident demonstrated even more dramatically than Three Mile Island the need for a higher level of training for nuclear operators, because it is difficult to believe that a well-trained and professional crew would have deliberately inactivated the safety devices built into the system.[9]

How Safe Are Reactors?

In 1979 an extensive study of the typical kinds of reactors used in this country documented the low probability of a serious nuclear accident. The study, commissioned by the Nuclear Regulatory Commission and known as the Rasmussen report, concluded that if the United States operated as many as 200 nuclear reactors, the chances of a serious radioactive leak from one reactor would be so low as to be expected only once in 10,000 years.[10] Since there have been no serious reactor leaks as yet in the United States, not to mention fatalities, the prediction of the Rasmussen report still holds true. Considering that the report was written when safety precautions were less extensive than they are today, the report may actually overestimate the danger considerably.

But how is the safety record of reactors versus other kinds of fuels? In 1950 alone, some 600 coal miners died on the job; about 20,000 were injured. Vastly improved safety measures and the employment of 70,000 safety inspectors in the coal industry reduced fatalities to approximately 100 in 1975, still significant by any standard. But the enhanced safety was accomplished by increasing production costs and decreasing productivity, and the casualty figures do not include additional deaths and injuries caused by coal transportation and coal-fired power plant operation.[11]

All told, coal mine accidents have killed a staggering 90,000 miners since 1907. Even with today's increased safety, coal mine deaths average 260 per year with another several thousand deaths each

[9]Atwood.

[10]Jack J. Kraushaar and Robert A. Ristinen, *Energy and Problems of a Technical Society*, rev. ed. (New York: John Wiley and Sons, 1988), pp. 135–37.

[11]Charles A. S. Hall et al. *Energy and Resource Quality* (New York: John Wiley and Sons, 1986), pp. 246–48.

year attributed to maladies such as black lung disease.[12] Compared
to that monumental toll, even the Chernobyl accident pales into
insignificance. Yet there has been no groundswell of public opinion
to eliminate coal-fired power plants. Herbert Inhaber, writing in
Science, studied the relative risks associated with the various means
of electric power generation. He estimated 3,000 total person-days
were lost per megawatt year for coal-fired plants, 2,000 for oil-fired
plants, and 10 for nuclear plants. If these figures are roughly correct,
and there is no reason to believe that they are not, then the major
alternatives to nuclear power are themselves 200–300 times more
risky than nuclear power.[13]

The nuclear power industry could help assure the public of its
safety by calling for the repeal of the Price-Anderson Act, under
which the federal government limits the nuclear plant operators'
liability in accidents. If the industry had to rely entirely on unsubsi-
dized private insurance, many concerned people would be put at
ease.[14]

The Nuclear Waste Question

Besides the fear of the nuclear plant itself, the other rallying point
of the anti-nuclear activists is the disposal of radioactive wastes
from operation of the plant. Waste arises because the uranium 235
becomes spent and no longer supports fission. The spent fuel rods
must be replaced and disposed of. The rods are by no means benign;
they contain elements such as plutonium, which has a half-life (the
time needed for a radioactive substance to decay to one-half of its
original activity) of 24,000 years. But most of the elements in these
rods have relatively short half-lives. Therefore, much of the radioactivity of the rods can be dissipated by storing them in water for a
few years, after which the remaining uranium and plutonium can
be reclaimed by reprocessing. The water storage serves to eliminate
those radioactive substances with short half-lives, but does not
eliminate the activity of the remaining uranium or plutonium.
Those remaining wastes can then be made into a solid, combined

[12]David M. Gates, p. 127.

[13]Herbert Inhaber, "Risk with Energy from Conventional and Nonconventional
Sources," *Science*, February 23, 1979, p. 718.

[14]See Barry P. Brownstein, "The Price-Anderson Act: Is It Consistent with a Sound
Energy Policy?" *Policy Analysis* no. 36 (Washington: Cato Institute, April 17, 1984).

with glass frits, and sent to a waste depository. Such was the original disposal plan, which, because of mismanagement by the Atomic Energy Commission (AEC) and pressures by anti-nuclear groups, has been halted.

The Atomic Energy Act of 1954 charged the AEC with encouraging the development of a competitive industry for nuclear energy power generation. AEC officials felt that reprocessing would make nuclear energy more competitive by reducing fuel costs. They even offered to buy the recovered plutonium as an additional incentive to reprocessing. Operating under AEC economic guarantees, the Nuclear Fuel Services Company built a reprocessing plant at West Valley, New York, in 1962 and began operating in 1966. To keep prices low enough to make reprocessing more appealing to electric utilities, the AEC encouraged Nuclear Fuel to minimize capital expenditures. The resulting design of the reprocessing plant led to inadequate ventilation, improper shielding, and elimination of a number of safety features.[15] The plant was also too small to exploit economies of scale.

By 1972 and in the face of large losses, Nuclear Fuel closed its plant, ostensibly to enlarge it for more efficient operation. The AEC began hearings on the proposed expansion, at which time the Sierra Club, other environmentalists, and even plant employees complained about unsafe conditions. As a result of those hearings, the AEC mandated modifications that would have cost $600 million as compared to the $32 million cost of the original plant. As a result, Nuclear Fuel withdrew from the industry.

In the meantime Allied General had begun to build a reprocessing plant at Barnwell, South Carolina. The Sierra Club and the Natural Resources Defense Council used their legal expertise to obtain a series of court orders that stopped completion of the facility. In 1976, President Gerald Ford administered the coup de grace by declaring a three-year moratorium on reprocessing. President Jimmy Carter's indefinite ban brought to an end the most promising solution for handling nuclear wastes.

The fear that the plutonium from reprocessing would fall into the hands of terrorists was the stated driving force behind presidential bans on reprocessing. Yet France (which generates 65 percent

---

[15]Campbell, pp. 110–22.

of its electricity power by nuclear means), England, India, and Japan have used reprocessing technology for years with no reports of misadventure. By not reprocessing, the United States is confronted with the problem of having to store a much larger quantity of nuclear wastes safely and doing so without disturbance or leakage into the soil or ground water for the thousands of years of plutonium's half-life. The plutonium, which has enormous value as fuel in its own right, is completely wasted. Its removal by reprocessing would cut the storage time needed for the longest-lived nuclear waste product to 600 years. Meanwhile spent fuel rods are being stored in rapidly filling ponds near the nation's nuclear reactors, and $2 billion is being spent simply to study the feasibility of using Yucca Mountain in Nevada as a suitable waste storage site. The full cost of the Yucca Mountain project, with its honeycomb of tunnels within the mountain, is expected to be about $35 billion. Of course, Nevada's environmentalists are rallying round a new battle cry, "No Nukes in Nevada!" The NIMBY (not in my back yard) syndrome is most virulent in the nuclear disposal issue.

Even the physical magnitude of the waste disposal problem is exaggerated in the mind of the public. With reprocessing, the annual high-level waste from a 1,000-megawatt nuclear reactor would occupy a cubic volume of about 9 feet on a side, a volume that might be stored in a large broom closet. In fact, with reprocessing, all nonmilitary reactors now operating in the United States would produce an annual volume of high-level wastes equal to about 35 feet on a side.[16]

Is a Successful Program Possible?

We cannot cover all the good ideas for a successful nuclear program. Nevertheless, the French program hints at what might be done here.

The French place great stock in their independence. As a result, they were able to reach a national political understanding that, given their limited supply of coal and petroleum, they should have a large nuclear power industry. To that end, the French nuclear industry concentrated on standardization. Electricité de France (EDF) is treated as a national monopoly and is able to design its

---

[16]Kraushaar and Ristinen, p. 146.

own plants and to designate one firm, Framatome, to do all the construction. Another company monopolizes all spent-fuel reprocessing. By contrast, each nuclear power plant in the United States is generally a unique creation. Design certification is required for each new unit. The U.S. method of design and construction is largely motivated by the power companies' fear that they would run afoul of our antitrust laws if they "conspired" to standardize nuclear power plants. The continued need for certification creates long delays in construction in the United States, delays that are not experienced by the French. As a result, U.S. nuclear power plants require longer periods of finance before they can earn any revenue; that drives up capital costs enormously. Of course, there are other reasons for construction delays, some of which can conceivably be open-ended—construction can be stopped almost indefinitely by court orders, politicians in need of an issue, or protesters' bodies in the road.

The United States need not create monopolies as the French did. It need only grant exemptions from antitrust law for nuclear power plant design and construction to allow standardization. One would think that with the passage of time and technological advances, such exemptions would become moot for nuclear electrical generation. (For example, the development of a miniature nuclear reactor that was as safe as any other home appliance would likely make any "natural monopoly" in nuclear electric power generation obsolete.) Without the initial exemptions, however, technology may never be able to progress at all.[17]

But legal changes to allow standardization are not enough. The French national commitment also meant that the major political parties have agreed to keep the issue out of the political arena. France does not have the open hearings one finds in the United States, where political and environmental groups can gain the attention of the media by "revealing" new nuclear dangers. Without the grandstanding, debate in France is probably more thoughtful

---

[17]For a discussion of the competitive nature of electric utilities, see John C. Moorehouse, ed., *Electric Power: Deregulation and the Public Interest* (San Francisco: Pacific Research Institute for Public Policy, 1986); Robert W. Poole, Jr., ed., *Unnatural Monopolies: The Case for Deregulating Public Utilities* (Lexington: Lexington Books, 1985); and Walter J. Primeaux, Jr., *Direct Electric Utility Competition: The Natural Monopoly Myth* (New York: Praeger, 1986).

than many of the public spectacles of U.S. hearings. It would be better still to remove the nuclear energy issues from the political arena entirely.

Fossil fuels are clearly more damaging to the environment and to mankind than nuclear fuel. Nuclear power alone is capable of carrying mankind well into the next century when, perhaps, technology will have produced an even better alternative. If the nation is bold enough to permit private development of breeder nuclear reactors, which manufacture plutonium, U.S. energy needs could be satisfied for thousands of years into the future.

The major difficulties with nuclear power relate, once again, to irrational fears that are abetted by sensational media attention. An oil refinery explosion that kills 10 people barely makes the national news; the accidental discharge of steam from a nuclear power plant becomes a media circus. A huge cost is exacted: higher electric bills, stockholder disenchantment with the electric utility industry, and the decreased ability of U.S. producers to compete internationally. The continued needless destruction of the environment and dependence on foreign fuel supplies, which could again easily lead us into war, are unpardonable.

10. Conclusion

In the 1920s and 1930s, when large numbers of American and European intellectuals were asserting that communism would soon defeat capitalism, the Viennese economist Ludwig von Mises dissented. Mises knew, as do all economists, that every resource is scarce and must somehow be rationed. Capitalism rations by means of market prices while socialism hopes to ration by means of enlightened bureaucrats. Mises pointed out that no matter how well-meaning, benevolent, or intelligent the bureaucrats might be, they were doomed to fail because of the lack of market-generated prices.

The process of allowing people to engage in free exchange generates information in the form of relative prices; that information indicates what should be produced. Such information, for example, guided the movement of resources out of the buggy whip industry and into the accelerator pedal business with the invention of the automobile. The information contained in relative prices, Mises said, is indispensable to the operation of an efficient economy and cannot be gotten in any way other than by permitting free exchange. Since socialism and communism cannot, by their very definition, tolerate the free-market process, those systems are bound to fail.

The ongoing collapse of socialism everywhere in the world has certainly vindicated Mises. Soviet planners desperately attempted to allocate resources with some modicum of efficiency by using German prices, but they failed; German prices were not Soviet prices. What industrial production there was seemed to be the most ecologically destructive in the world.

Information and Innovation

If information is essential to the short-run allocation of resources, it is also essential for long-term economic progress. Students of economic development have searched for years to identify the reasons why some countries are rich while others are poor. The best answer these scholars can come up with is that nations that grow rich have an economic and political system that allows people to be innovative. Economic historians Nathan Rosenberg and E. L. Birdzell put it as follows: "The immediate sources of Western growth were innovations in trade, technology, and organization. . . . [Innovation is] virtually an additional factor of production."[1]

For an innovation to have any effect on society, it must be brought to the attention of the people of that society—it must be brought to market. The market economies of the West have adopted a kind of insurance, or risk-spreading, system by allowing many firms and individuals to innovate; the decision about any innovation never rests on the shoulders of a few decisionmakers. The freedom to innovate, to bring an innovation to market, and to reap the rewards is the single clear thread that runs through the history of economic growth. And as we have stressed throughout this book, the wealth that results from economic growth is the single clearest determinant of both the good life and the good environment. The environment does not take precedence over the economy, nor vice versa. The two are locked in vital dependence on one another.

Proper communication of information is unquestionably one of the most important elements in a free, prosperous, and environmentally satisfying society. Unfortunately, the American people are not receiving good information on which to base competent decisions. The market for new innovations, for example, is blocked increasingly by needless regulation that is engendered by fear, often created out of whole cloth by the media or by academics who forget that the first duty of a scientist is to tell the truth, the whole truth, and nothing but the truth without regard for political biases.[2]

When our media create hysteria over, for example, the safety of new drugs, people often forget that invention and innovation in the drug industry will be slowed by the greater regulation that such hysteria generally brings in its train. The upshot is that fewer new drugs will be brought to market, and those that are finally brought

[1]Nathan Rosenberg and L. E. Birdzell, *How the West Grew Rich* (New York: Basic Books, 1986) p. 20.

[2]Sheldon Krimsky and Alonzo Plough have written a book on the problem of accurate communication of risk, *Environmental Hazards: Communicating Risks as a Social Process* (Dover, Mass.: Auburn House, 1988). Needless to say, these scientists are not able to offer a good answer as to how accurate information on environmental risks can be communicated within the context of the media as they exist today.

will be both slower to arrive and more expensive. As AIDS sufferers have been quick to point out in recent years, lives can be lost because of that slowness and expense. Even former Food and Drug Administration commissioner Arthur Hull Hayes is said to have wondered out loud whether the FDA could be changed so that it not only protected but actually benefited the public as well.[3] Perhaps a new slogan is needed: "Regulation Kills!"

Science and Stories

When scientists get together, they talk about "stories," which is their way of referring to explanations for phenomena that interest them. Science could well be characterized as an enterprise that is never satisfied with the current story and that tries to improve on it. The good people in science are always uncertain whether their explanation is the correct one for any given phenomenon; they know full well that no story is ever complete.

For the most part, scientists are able to explain a phenomenon only after the fact. Accurate prediction of events that have never been known to happen before is extremely rare, so much so that it usually results in a Nobel Prize. Only slightly more common is science's success at predicting quasi-repetitive phenomena (earthquakes and business cycles) that have happened before and may, under the right circumstances, happen again. In the case of the ozone "hole," one scientific story can be created that "explains" it in terms of some synthetic chemical and another story can be created that "explains" it in terms of, say, volcanic activity. The stories need not be mutually exclusive; both may contain truth or they both may be entirely false. Nevertheless, the "hole" was not predicted by science. If it should vanish or change drastically in scope, that probably will not have been predicted either.

The intelligent layperson's responsibility is to evaluate scientific stories, and, as we have tried to point out in this book, people should never be afraid of applying common sense to that enterprise. Nor should anyone be surprised when scientists themselves are the last to see the common sense of an argument opposing their latest story, since they are as apt as anyone to be blinded by love of their own creation.

[3]Daniel Henninger, "Will the FDA Revert to Type?" *Wall Street Journal*, December 12, 1990, p. A18.

What is perhaps different about science today is that we have allowed ourselves to be paralyzed by the fear that industry *might* create something that will harm us in the extreme. We live under something that *Atlantic* magazine has dubbed "laboratory-mouse terrorism." We are, collectively, like the patient of Carl Jung, who lived in constant fear of cancer. Jung wrote:

> I recall a professor of philosophy who once consulted me about his cancer phobia. He suffered from a compulsive conviction that he had a malignant tumor, although nothing of the kind was ever found in dozens of X-ray pictures. "Oh, I know there is nothing," he would say, "but there *might* be something."[4]

To be sure, irrational fears of scientific advances and industrial techniques have existed before. Lightning rods were at one time outlawed in parts of the United States for fear that the ground itself would become so filled with electricity that crops would die. Yet lightning rods were not outlawed everywhere, and experience with them in one part of the country put irrational fears concerning their use to rest in other parts. Today, however, national regulatory agencies have made it possible for us to outlaw or simply abandon a scientific advance or an industrial technique everywhere, merely on the grounds that some group convinced an important media personality of potential harm. The Alar case is a good example. Somehow people have not yet come to grips with the fact that this situation represents raw power that is probably greater than that held by anyone in the industrial sector. The media, from *Time* magazine to NBC, are no longer reporters on the environment but advocates of environmental causes. As Andrea Mitchell of NBC was quoted as saying, "Clearly, the networks have made that decision now, where you'd have to call it advocacy."[5] Indeed, journalists have been urged by political leaders such as Vice President Albert Gore to avoid confusing the public with environment stories that are not alarming.[6]

---

[4] Carl G. Jung, "Approaching the Unconscious," in *Man and His Symbols*, ed. C. G. Jung and M.-L. von Franz (New York: Doubleday, 1964), p. 47. Italics in original.

[5] *AIM Report*, October-A, 1990, p. 1.

[6] Gregg Easterbrook, "Green Cassandras," *New Republic*, July 6, 1992, pp. 23–25.

The reality is that it is no longer possible to undertake any clear and rational economic or political analysis of what is right with the environment, given the interaction of bureaucracy, the media, and the resulting politicizing of environmental issues. Any political move to reduce the costs of some environmental program (such as was clearly called for under the NAPAP report on acid rain) is characterized by the media as an assault on the environment. Results do not count, only the amount of money spent. And when a man enters the White House with the desire to become the "environmental" president, it takes even less media criticism to cause the money and regulation spigots to be opened.

Economics, Politics, and Regulation

There are basically four ways to deal with pollution: the market approach, the common law approach, the private voluntary action approach, and the government regulation approach.[7] None of these approaches is perfect and, realistically, all will probably need to be used should the taste for environmental amenities continue to increase among the American people.

The market approach has much to recommend it if a way can be found to use it. For a very simple example of this approach, consider a firm that produces both milk and cow manure in its dairy operation. If no market exists for the manure, the firm has produced a pollutant, pure and simple. However, if some market can be made for cow manure, then the pollutant can become a valuable product such as fertilizer. The pollutant has been transformed by the market into a resource.

An interesting thing about the market approach is that it can play a very flexible and dynamic role in creating economic growth. As relative scarcities develop in certain resources, the market will tend to identify uses for things that were once thought to be nuisances. An increase in the price of silver, for example, caused the photographic industry to invest in recovery equipment that removed silver from film-processing waste water.

---

[7]See, for example, Joseph J. Seneca and Michael K. Taussig, *Environmental Economics*, 2d ed. (Englewood Cliffs, N.J.: Prentice-Hall, 1979).

The related common law or property rights approach also has much to recommend it.[8] Under common law, people have for generations had the right to redress harm done to them or their property. If someone infringes on your personal or property rights by polluting, you have the right to sue for damages or, under dire conditions, to obtain prior restraint from the courts. The great strengths of the common law approach are that it uses a system of justice that attempts to identify the rights of the parties to the action.[9]

The common law approach relies on the principle of accountability, which is held in low esteem among many segments of society. But the common law can be slow to give relief. Further, the approach can require a level of proof of damage that is missing in the claims of many environmentalists. (Laws and regulations have been passed that make it entirely too easy to allege harm—it does not take much for a regulatory agency to find danger, egged on by some political interest group. Much is done in the name of what John Shelton Reed called, after Veblen, "conspicuous benevolence."[10])

Nevertheless, economists widely agree that property rights must be expanded as a method of controlling pollution. People, like puppies, refrain from fouling their own nests. Where fishing rights are owned, overfishing ceases to be a problem. Companies that own their own forests are careful about replanting after harvesting. Richard L. Stroup offers this example:

> Consider England and Scotland, where sports and commercial fishing rights are privately owned and transferable. Access is often rented daily or leased for longer terms, and prices vary from a few dollars per month for bait fishing to very high fees for the rarest and finest fly fishing. Long before the environmental movement took hold, owners of

---

[8]See Tibor R. Machan, "Capitalism and the Environment," *Freeman*, July 1990, pp. 249–57, for an exposition of the Lockean versus the utilitarian view of market control. Machan recognizes the critical problem of the definition of pollution. Another advocate of this approach is Richard L. Stroup, "Environmental Policy," *Regulation*, 1988 no. 2, pp. 43–49.

[9]See Richard L. Stroup, "Environmental Policy," *Regulation*, 1988, pp. 43–9.

[10]John Shelton Reed, "Letter from the Lower Right," *Chronicles*, September 1990, pp. 44–45.

fishing rights successfully sued polluters of streams for damages and obtained injunctions against polluting activities. It worked: now they seldom have to go to court. Polluters generally leave those waters (and thus the fish) alone. When resources are owned, political wars are no longer necessary to protect them.[11]

Or consider the example given by Fred L. Smith, Jr.:

An excellent example of how private property better reconciles environmental and economic values is the Rainey Wildlife Refuge. This refuge, owned by a major environmental group, is located in the midst of vast natural gas and oil fields. Since the refuge was privately owned, development was at the discretion of the environmental group, the National Audubon Society. That "purist attitude," however, would have lost the royalty payments of a producing well. The Society elected to permit drilling under careful guidelines to reduce environmental damage. Economic and environmental gains to all resulted. In contrast, the Audubon Society, along with most other U.S. environmental organizations, vigorously opposes any energy development in a politically controlled Arctic National Wildlife Refuge. Absent a property stake in rational development, there is little reason to be rational.[12]

The common law and market approaches are not mutually exclusive. In fact, they reinforce each other admirably. Common law tends to bubble up from the bottom of society; it is invented by people as needed rather than legislated from above. As markets appear and mature, common law also appears and matures. We are sometimes not even aware that common law exists around us since it is enforced by markets themselves rather than by courts. Untold amounts of money are involved each day in stock exchange transactions that are based entirely on oral promises. People who cannot deliver on their promises are excluded from future trading. Since such exclusion deprives those people of their livelihoods, the sanction is quite powerful, and amazingly few promises are broken.

[11]Stroup, pp. 48–49.

[12]Fred L. Smith, Jr., "A Free Market Environmental Program," *Cato Journal*, Winter 1992, p. 465.

Private voluntary action has a long and honored history in environmental preservation and improvement in the United States. Ducks Unlimited has no doubt done as much to improve the habitat of wild ducks as has any governmental agency. Yet this organization receives little credit from environmentalists because its motives are not "pure": the organization's aim is to shoot the ducks once they have grown. The point is that private voluntary action involves a market for environmental goods. People who want to hunt ducks or catch trout voluntarily invest money and time to promote those ends.

The basic difficulty with government regulation is that it tends to be rule-based with no positive incentives for the polluter to "clean up his act." Government regulation tends to lock in technology. If a polluter installs expensive technology, both the polluter and the regulator are reluctant to change to a new technology. Government regulation of pollution by rule making is the equivalent of the static command-and-control economic system that has led to such tragic consequences in Soviet-type economies. Clearly, environmental goods should not be produced in the same way that the Soviet Union made shoes.

Most economists recommend that when government regulation cannot be avoided, it should act to "internalize" the social costs of pollution by setting up programs that mimic a market system. The idea is that the regulators should not mandate that a particular technology be installed to prevent pollution, because the regulators do not know better than the individuals involved how best to abate pollution. Rather, a fee would be charged for pollution. Two practical problems are that the level of the fee might become politicized and the more radical environmentalists will argue that no price can be set on pollution. The objection to setting a price for an optimal level of pollution is a variation of the attitude that there can be no end to cleaning the environment, an attitude that is prevalent among some segments of the environmental movement. Nevertheless, in situations where pollution can be measured fairly easily (as in discharges from factories), the pricing method is vastly superior to a command-and-control approach simply because it allows the polluter the flexibility to choose the cheapest way of abating the pollution. A study done in the Delaware estuary, for example, has estimated that the costs of pollution abatement by effluent charges would be about half that of direct controls.[13]

To understand the superiority of pollution charges over technology mandates, one must consider that pollution exists because environmental goods such as clean air and water have not been priced. It is in everybody's individual best interest to make use of "free" goods. People who pollute are not bad people, just people who know a bargain when they see it. Under regulatory programs that are technology-based, delay can bring great benefits. The individual who is regulated can claim that the standard is impossible to meet, that it will cause bankruptcy, or that it is not the best technology available. Under a system of charges, the chances of delay are much less since the charges can be levied even as they are being battled in the courts.

Of course, all those methods of pollution control depend critically on the definition of pollution, something that we argue is not being provided to the people of the United States. Nevertheless, despite the lack of good information on just what pollution is, one can still argue that a combination of common law and market orientation will offer superior results to a command-and-control approach of government regulation. We say this for six reasons:

First, as we have contended, it is not at all clear that government rule makers are competent to determine better than markets and individuals do which things are environmentally damaging. In fact, the single outstanding characteristic of government rules is that they politicize environmental issues and increase the size and scope of the government. The rules are touted as being beneficent, but as Justice Brandeis warned several decades ago:

> Experience should teach us to be most on guard to protect liberty when the governments' purposes are beneficent. Men born to freedom are naturally alert to repel invasion of their liberty by evil-minded rulers. The greatest dangers to liberty lurk in insidious encroachments by men of zeal, well-meaning but without understanding.[14]

[13]Larry E. Ruff, "The Economic Common Sense of Pollution," in *Economics of the Environment*, 2d ed., ed. Robert Dorfman and Nancy S. Dorfman (New York: W.W. Norton, 1977), pp. 41–58.

[14]As quoted in Robert A. Nisbet, "The New Despotism," in *The Politicization of Society*, ed. Kenneth S. Templeton, Jr. (Indianapolis: Liberty Press, 1979), pp. 169–207.

Second, a rule-making authority not only distorts the information of the market, as we have argued, but it interacts with that information in unpredictable ways. Political interest groups can sue, or threaten to sue, the bureaucrats, forcing them to enforce laws in ways never intended by the legislators, who may have passed the law merely to curry political favor and with the hope that it would never be enforced.

Third, there is little or no evidence that bureaucrats protect either the people or the environment better than the market does. It has generally been assumed that market failure can be counteracted by government intervention and that the government is interested only in the public good. The economist and Nobel laureate James Buchanan has helped put to rest the notion that bureaucrats can save us from market failure; he has demonstrated that markets do not fail as often as was once thought, and that bureaucrats tend to look after their own self-interest first, in the same way everybody else does. Further, as we have argued, the process of regulation itself may cause market failure, and government regulatory failure can be indeterminately more expensive than the most expensive market failure—the example of the savings and loan regulatory debacle and government deposit insurance should suffice to illustrate that point.

One should never forget that bureaucrats are paid, for the most part, in proportion to how many people they manage. It is, therefore, in the best interests of the bureaucrats themselves to maximize the size of their organizations. What better way to accomplish this feat than to create a crisis that requires greater regulation and, naturally, a larger staff? Left-wing capitalism-bashers like John Kenneth Galbraith have long accused business of manipulating people into buying products that they did not really need or want. Whether or not the charge is true, that is how bureaucrats behave today with respect to environmental "products." An essential difference is that those needless products are paid for by taxpayers at large, the manipulated and the nonmanipulated alike.

Fourth, government regulation of the environment can be extremely expensive not only in environmental results per dollar but, as we have pointed out, in terms of future economic growth, which is the basic source of future environmental improvement. A small story of the interaction of hysteria and regulation conspiring to saddle the economy with tremendous costs should suffice. In September 1987, a government hazardous materials "expert" closed Interstate 5 at San Diego for several hours while protecting the public from a "hazardous substance" spill. Two 65-foot cleanup trucks were dispatched to retrieve a 50-pound bag of a reddish-brown substance that had been classified by the government as hazardous and toxic: iron oxide, also known as rust.[15] In this and many other cases, the world would have been better off had the government stayed out of the matter completely but, of course, in the current intellectual atmosphere of regulation feeding on hysteria, the government will not stay out.

Fifth, we need to mention again the problem of the unintended consequences resulting from inadequate knowledge. States such as California and Florida, for example, have adopted land-use regulation that, among other things, is intended to preserve the environment—especially environmental beauty. Generally, what these laws do is to promote "balancing"—a developer wants to build 100 housing units in a given space and the regulator negotiates this number down to, say, 50.[16] Such negotiation not only makes each housing unit more expensive, but it also tends to spread the units out farther, leading to more urban sprawl and more gasoline consumption by people who have been prevented by regulation from living nearer to their work. The land has been prevented from reaching its highest and best use according to the market, and it is not at all clear that anything positive has been accomplished, even in improving the beauty of the area.

Finally, there is what economists call rent-seeking, an example of which is the support of regulation that will bring the supporter monetary returns that could not be otherwise obtained. This counterproductive activity is obviously one reason for support of new environmental initiatives. Gary Anderson, among others, traces much of the early pure food and drug legislation, which led to the formation of the Food and Drug Administration, to firms attempting to gain advantages over competitors.[17]

---

[15]See Ben Bolch and Harold Lyons, "Not All 'Scares' of the EPA Fit the Facts," *Memphis Commercial Appeal*, February 25, 1989, p. B12.

[16]See Bernard H. Siegan, "Land Use Regulation Should Preserve Only Vital and Pressing Governmental Interests, *Cato Journal*, Spring/Summer 1990, pp. 127–58.

[17]Gary M. Anderson, "Parasites, Profits, and Politicians: Public Health and Public Choice," *Cato Journal*, Winter 1990, pp. 557–78.

127

Rent-seeking continues today as corn growers and gas producers lobby for alcohol additives in gasoline as a method of reducing carbon dioxide, a greenhouse gas. Ethanol from corn was first touted as a way to deal with the energy crisis until it was pointed out that more energy might be needed to produce that kind of fuel than could ever be released by it. Ethanol also would require more arable land than is available on the earth to grow the biomass needed to make enough to power the existing motor vehicle fleet. Now it and methanol come as saviors of the environment under the Clean Air Amendments of 1990. Methanol, or wood alcohol, is so toxic that it can cause death by merely being spilled on one's body. (We wonder if it could have been advocated by anyone other than an environmentalist.) Methanol is produced by partially burning a perfectly good fuel (natural gas). When that processing is taken into account, it is questionable whether less carbon dioxide would be released per mile driven by methanol than by gasoline.[18]

Still, it is an ill wind that blows no one any good, and the United States is currently supporting continental farmers by importing European wine through the Virgin Islands and turning it into automotive-fuel ethanol. For the scientific community, the Clean Air Amendments contain numerous research goodies, including $19 million to study cow flatulence.[19] Everybody seems to benefit from rent-seeking except the ordinary taxpayer.

Philosophy and Life

We pointed out earlier that life expectancy is now so great in the United States that it is doubtful that any improvement in our environment will have a great impact on increasing it much beyond the present level. People virtually never live beyond 120 years of age no matter what their environment, and a life much better than that of an invalid is rare beyond the age of 90. Therefore, under present technology, it is doubtful that we can achieve another doubling of life expectancy over the next 150 years. We seem to have biological clocks within us that simply run their allotted schedules,

[18] Ben Bolch and Harold Lyons, "Alternative Fuels Are Poor Choices," *Memphis Commercial Appeal*, May 20, 1990, p. B6.

[19] James J. Kilpatrick, "$19 Million for Flatulent Cows," *Human Events*, December 1, 1990, p. 15.

and there is little that present-day science can do to extend them.[20] Increasingly, it is becoming clear to biological scientists that if life expectancy is to be extended very much, it must be done by tinkering with these clocks directly. Even popular columnists such as Ellen Goodman are beginning to get the message that it may not be so much what we eat or the environment in which we live that determines life expectancy, but rather family history—we need to be sure to choose parents who are both rich and healthy![21]

Yet the philosophy of life Americans have embraced in recent years attempts to place the blame for disease and death on fatty foods, lack of exercise, industrial products, or the environment in general. Cancer and many other diseases are often no longer thought of as natural phenomena. By blaming and banning products before the phenomena and the unintended consequences of the ban are understood, the regulators risk causing large numbers of deaths that would not have occurred otherwise.

The realization that the philosophy of environmental zealots is itself destructive is essential to an understanding of the environmental movement. Robert Bidinotto, in an excellent exposition of the link between the environmental movement and the socialist-redistributionists, distinguishes between Greens and Deep Ecologists in the following way: "[Greens] . . . want to rid the planet of rich people, and the Deep Ecologists . . . want to rid the planet of people, period."[22] Like Bidinotto, it is perhaps time for people to assert, without shame, that they favor a philosophy that is blatantly anthropocentric.

A Religion of Fear

Newsweek has declared that young people are returning to religion.[23] Ordinarily we would view that as a hopeful sign except that one of the religions listed is "Deep Ecology." Still, that great American clergyman, Ralph Waldo Emerson, knew that nature

[20]S. Jay Olshansky et al., "In Search of Methuselah: Estimating the Upper Limits of Human Longevity," *Science*, November 2, 1990, pp. 634–40.

[21]Ellen Goodman, "Not Necessarily Equal," *Memphis Commercial Appeal*, December 11, 1990, p. A9.

[22]Robert James Bidinotto, "Environmentalism: Freedom's Foe for the '90s." *Freeman*, November 1990, p. 418.

[23]*Newsweek*, December 17, 1990, p. 54.

wore the "colors of the spirit."[24] What is glorious and beautiful one minute becomes corrupted and hideous the next, all depending on the lightness of the observer's heart. Much environmentalism is a counsel of fear and despair that advises the forfeiture of income, wealth, freedom, and even life to prevent such a far-fetched terror as global warming. Why? Because, like Armageddon, the consequences are simply too terrible to contemplate.

This attempt to convince by fear and intimidation is one of the surest of all tip-offs that the issue being discussed is not the environment but rather some hidden agenda: a new utopia. Why else must the burden of proof fall on those who would preserve freedom rather than on those who would take it away? How else could the gift of democratic capitalism, which has given us nothing less than the revolutionary enhancement of human life and the elimination of starvation and abject poverty, be damned by those purveyors of melancholy?[25] Like other collectivist utopians before them, environmentalists feel the need, in Karl Popper's words, to clean the canvas before they paint the beautiful picture of their new order.[26] But unlike their predecessors, the utopians wish to erase more than institutions and ideas; they wish to erase people as well. What they fail to realize is that in the process of canvas cleaning, they will also erase themselves.

It is all too easy to become depressed by these messianic "defenders" of the environment, but that attitude must be resisted. Mises, we remember, was a prescient thinker who in the midst of the rise of both Soviet and Nazi socialism (calamities among the greatest ever faced by mankind) refused to be a pessimist. He wrote:

> The main error of this widespread pessimism is the belief that the destructionist ideas and policies of our age sprang from the proletarians and are a "revolt of the masses." In fact, the masses, precisely because they are not creative and do not develop philosophies of their own, follow the leaders. The ideologies which produced all the mischiefs and catastrophes of our century are not an achievement of

[24]See his essay "Nature."

[25]Michael Novak, in *The Spirit of Democratic Capitalism* (New York: Simon & Schuster, 1982), asks the questions of theologians in a much more elegant way.

[26]Karl R. Popper, *The Open Society and Its Enemies: The Spell of Plato* (Princeton, N.J.: Princeton University Press, 1971), p. 167.

the mob. They are the feat of pseudo-scholars and pseudo-intellectuals. They were propagated from the chairs of universities and from the pulpit, they were disseminated by the press, by novels and plays and by the movies and the radio. The intellectuals converted the masses to socialism and interventionism. These ideologies owe the power they have today to the fact that all means of communication have been turned over to their supporters and almost all dissenters have been virtually silenced. What is needed to turn the flood is to change the mentality of the intellectuals.[27]

For the sake of both mankind and the environment, we hope that such a change will be soon in coming.

---

[27]Ludwig von Mises, "The Political Chances of Genuine Liberalism," in *Planning for Freedom* (Spring Mills, Pa.: Libertarian Press, 1980), p. 181.

Index

in Western industrialized nations,
35–36
Environmental disasters, 33
Environmental movement
anthropomorphism of nature in,
21–22
to limit or ban human activity, 9–11
manipulation by, 18, 20, 22–23
reasons for backlash against, 10–12
theories of, 5–8
See also Deep ecology; Earth First!;
Ecoterrorism; Green movement
Environmental Protection Agency
(EPA)
asbestos removal policy, 57
costs of compliance with rules of, vii
estimate of Alar risk, 41–43
estimates of dioxin toxicity, 60–61
in prediction of radon health effects,
63, 66–70
role in banning chemicals, 40
scientific opposition to, 69–70
Eppley Institute, 40
Ethanol, 128
Eugenics, 37

Feinstein, Alvin, 45
Fenton, David, 18
Fenton Communications Company, 39
Finnish Forest Research Service, 98–99
Fish disappearance argument, 100
Food additives, 41–43
See also Alar
Ford, Gerald, 112
Forest devastation argument, 97–99
Free chlorine, 89
Freedom, viii
Freudenthal, Ralph I., 40n3
Freudenthal, Susan L., 40n3
Frink, Charles, 95n2, 99, 100–101
Fulton, J. P., 51

Galbraith, John Kenneth, 126
Garcia, Rolando R., 86n4
Gates, David M., 108n6, 111n12
Georgescu-Roegen, Nicholas, 31
Glaciation, 76
Gleick, James, 72n2
Global warming
getting attention for, 80
news and warning of, 76–77
predicted evidence for and effects
of, 73, 78
Gold, Lois, 41, 42, 53
Goodman, Ellen, 129
Gore, Albert, 77, 81, 120
Government

assessment of risk by, 18
as source of cost assumption, 2, 24
See also Bureaucracy; Regulation
Greenhouse effect
computer models of, 74–76, 78,
79, 81
predictions related to, 73
Green movement, 8, 22, 129
Greenpeace, 22
Grossman, Henryk, 26n1

Hahn, Robert, 23
Hall, Charles A. S., 110n11
Hansen, James, 76–77
Hanson, David J., 60nn43,45, 61n48,
64n3, 66n6, 67n9
Harley, John, 69
Hayek, F. A., 22, 34
Hayes, Arthur Hull, 119
High Background Radiation Research
Group, 65
Hileman, Bette, 75–76
Himmelfarb, Milton, 37
Hixson, J., 53n25
Hoffer, Eric, 16, 20, 24
Hoffman, John, 77
Holm-Hansen, Osmond, 90
Hooker Chemical Company, 20, 58
Hormesis, 69
Horowitz, John K., 18n8
Houk, Vernon N., 61
Huang, Cliff, 46n13
Humphreys, W. J., 94
Hunter, Linda Mason, 63

Ice clouds, 79
Information
in free-market society, 117–18
in market system, 34
Inhaber, Herbert, 111
Innovation, 117–18

Jakubal, Mike, 4n6
Jastrow, Robert, 76, 79n22
Jones, Landon Y., 27n6
Jones, R. L., 88nn7,8
Jung, Carl, 5–6, 120

Kahn, Herman, 26n2
Kasun, Jacqueline, 32, 37
Kauppi, Pekka, 99n13
Kay, Jeanne, 6n13
Kelly, Allen, 36
Kemp, Jack, 11
Kerr, Richard A., 69n13, 72nn1,3,
75n8, 77nn13,14, 78n19, 80n23,
88n9, 89n10, 94nn21,22

About the Authors

Ben W. Bolch is the Robert D. McCallum Professor of Economics and Business Administration at Rhodes College in Memphis, Tennessee. He is a former chairman of the department of economics and business administration at Vanderbilt University. He received his Ph.D. from the University of North Carolina, Chapel Hill, and is the coauthor of two books on statistical inference that have been translated into several languages: *Practical Business Statistics* and *Multivariate Statistical Methods*. He has had papers published in the *Journal of the American Statistical Association, Review of Economics and Statistics, Southern Economic Journal,* and other scholarly publications.

Harold Lyons is the Schering Plough Professor of Chemistry, emeritus, at Rhodes College with a specialty in biochemistry and environmental chemistry. He was formerly the manager of analytical and physical chemical research in the research division of Koppers Co. He received his Ph.D. from Oklahoma State University. His scientific papers have been published in the *Journal of Surgical Research, Journal of Laboratory and Clinical Medicine, Experimental and Molecular Pathology,* and many other journals.

Cato Institute

Founded in 1977, the Cato Institute is a public policy research foundation dedicated to broadening the parameters of policy debate to allow consideration of more options that are consistent with the traditional American principles of limited government, individual liberty, and peace. To that end, the Institute strives to achieve greater involvement of the intelligent, concerned lay public in questions of policy and the proper role of government.

The Institute is named for *Cato's Letters*, libertarian pamphlets that were widely read in the American Colonies in the early 18th century and played a major role in laying the philosophical foundation for the American Revolution.

Despite the achievement of the nation's Founders, today virtually no aspect of life is free from government encroachment. A pervasive intolerance for individual rights is shown by government's arbitrary intrusions into private economic transactions and its disregard for civil liberties.

To counter that trend, the Cato Institute undertakes an extensive publications program that addresses the complete spectrum of policy issues. Books, monographs, and shorter studies are commissioned to examine the federal budget, Social Security, regulation, military spending, international trade, and myriad other issues. Major policy conferences are held throughout the year, from which papers are published thrice yearly in the *Cato Journal*. The Institute also publishes the quarterly magazine *Regulation.*

In order to maintain its independence, the Cato Institute accepts no government funding. Contributions are received from foundations, corporations, and individuals, and other revenue is generated from the sale of publications. The Institute is a nonprofit, tax-exempt, educational foundation under Section 501(c)3 of the Internal Revenue Code.

CATO INSTITUTE
1000 Massachusetts Ave., N.W.
Washington, D.C. 20001